D1337065

ABOUT THE AUTHOR

Michael Mulligan originates from the outskirts of Southend-on-Sea, Essex. As a teenager, he would buy as many as five music newspapers a week and could chart the growth of his music knowledge by his ability to complete the crossword puzzles.

In 1990, Mulligan got a job at his local record shop and spent the next twenty-five years working for all manner of music retailers. More recently, he has been a consultant for various record labels, mining their archives for overlooked gems. He has also authored several tie-in books for the successful *NOW! That's What I Call Music* brand.

Mulligan lives in north London with two cats, a patient and indulgent wife and an 'in no way too large' record collection.

NINE
EIGHT
BOOKS

NEB 001

First published in the UK in 2021 by Nine Eight Books
An imprint of Bonnier Books UK
4th Floor, Victoria House, Bloomsbury Square, London, WC1B 4DA
Owned by Bonnier Books, Sveavägen 56, Stockholm, Sweden

 @nineeightbooks

 @nineeightbooks

Hardback ISBN: 978-1-7887-0585-1

A CIP catalogue record for this book is available from the British Library.

Publishing director: Pete Selby
Senior editor: Melissa Bond

Design by David Pitt
Cover illustrations by Annie Arnold at Bonnier Books UK
Printed and bound in Poland

1 3 5 7 9 10 8 6 4 2

Nine Eight Books is an imprint of Bonnier Books UK
www.bonnierbooks.co.uk

FSC
www.fsc.org

MIX
Paper from
responsible sources
FSC® C018236

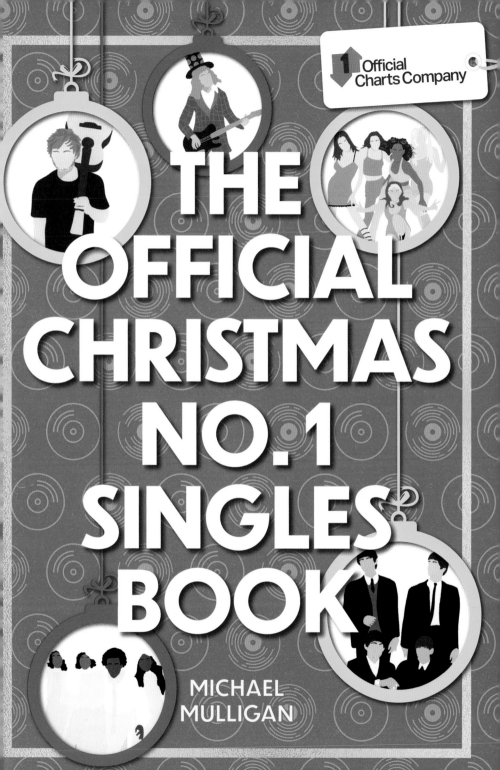

THE OFFICIAL CHRISTMAS NO.1 SINGLES BOOK

MICHAEL MULLIGAN

WELCOME TO THE OFFICIAL CHRISTMAS NO. 1 SINGLES BOOK

Welcome to *The Official Christmas No. 1 Singles Book* – an affectionate celebration of the good, the great and the occasionally curious recordings that provide a soundtrack to the festive season. Songs whose sales have been counted, listed and captured for posterity since the birth of the Official Singles Chart in 1952.

There is no other time of year when press, radio and television unfailingly report the chart-topping single as headline news; bookies even offer odds on the eventual Christmas number-one claimant. It is an event as keenly anticipated as the prospect of snow.

It seems songwriters and musicians feel a strange compulsion to create new songs for Christmas, though we can only guess as to whether this is driven by a warm festive glow or by the seasonal sales increase from shoppers buying gifts. With schools and businesses shut for the Christmas period, families have more leisure time on their hands, more time to spend together, more time to feel nostalgic and, crucially, more time to listen to music. Record labels, therefore, build their plans around the last few weeks of the year and hold back their big-hitters accordingly.

Shops, bars and restaurants accompany their decorations with a soundtrack of Yuletide melodies – a looped background of tinkling bells and cherubic choirs designed to put you in the right mood to part with your money. Indeed, Wizzard's 1973 single 'I Wish It Could Be Christmas Everyday' not only features bells and choirs, but even starts with the sound of a ringing till.

Perhaps music buyers feel more sentimental at Christmas? Could it be that the end of the year has them looking back and returning old favourites to the Official Chart? This is increasingly the case in recent years, as a simple tap of a button or command to a speaker can grant instant access to songs from every decade. Christmas music purchasers undoubtedly spare a thought for those less fortunate than them, too, which explains the number of chart-topping charity projects, although sometimes the great, unpredictable British public will buy a single just to stop another song getting to number one. What a strange and wonderful nation we are!

Encompassing solo artists, duos, boy bands, girl groups, comedians, choirs, charity collectives, talent shows, bloggers, vloggers, social media superstars and everything in between, this book will examine every Christmas number one to date (plus some songs that never quite made it to the top) and look at how, where and why music fans of the day bought the chart-topping singles they did. Our travels in trivia will also explore the evolution of the Official Chart itself – from 10-inch 78-rpm singles to instant-access online streaming, via 7-inch 45s, 12-inch extended mixes, cassette tapes, coloured vinyl, picture discs, compact discs and digital downloads. We will begin in an era when the Official Chart was the result of a newsdesk phone call to a handful of shops and we will end in the present day, with data now transmitted from more than 9,000 retailers, including sales from gleaming multinationals and cherished local independents alike, as well as download stores, streaming services and much more.

Along the way, we will encounter easy listening, rock 'n' roll, Merseybeat,

psychedelia, glam rock, prog rock, punk, new wave, New Romantics, soul, and dance, as well as comedy records, novelty songs, film soundtracks, television adverts – and maybe some common pop music, too. We will also ask – and hopefully answer – some important questions, like how many of our number ones were original songs and how many were cover versions? Which artist has had the most Christmas chart-toppers and which artists were one-hit wonders? Who was the youngest and who was the oldest? How many number ones actually mention Christmas and which chart-topper mentions the title of the song that knocked it off the top spot?

If your thoughts occasionally turn to eponymous number ones, posthumous number ones and instrumental number ones, then you're in good company. If you have ever paused to ponder 'how on earth did that get to be the Christmas chart-topper?', then this is definitely the place for you. And if you believe that there is no such thing as too much music trivia, then you will feel right at home with our fact-filled, fully illustrated *Official Christmas No. 1 Singles Book*.

In the words of Slade's Noddy Holder and Jim Lea, 'So here it is...'

WELCOME TO THE '50s

Welcome to the United Kingdom in the 1950s. Clothes rationing had ended in the final year of the previous decade, but fourteen years of food restrictions eventually came to a halt in July 1954. Those rushing out to buy provisions for a celebratory street party, though, should have been warned that conflict in the Middle East would result in the 1956 Suez Crisis, leading to shortages in petrol and petrol-based products – including records.

Although the seeds of the post-war 'baby boom' would take a few more years to mature, a recovering economy, growth in employment and a 'new' teenage demographic with disposable income and a desire to rebel against the previous generation – or possibly just enjoy themselves before another war started – would soon emerge. In the meantime, there were certainly no divisions in the music market.

National radio consisted of the BBC Home Service (mainly speech-based), the Light Programme (for light entertainment and popular music) and the Third Programme (for classical music and cricket commentary). The 'popular music' options included *Housewives' Choice*, the Band of the Welsh Guards on *Music While You Work*, Peter Keane at the BBC theatre organ, and Victor Silvester and His Ballroom Orchestra on *Music for Dancing*. The commercial alternative was Radio Luxembourg, though the differences were not always obvious. The station offered a home to programmes and performers who had fallen out with the BBC, including forces' sweetheart Vera Lynn.

Households lucky enough to own a television would have paid around £85 (equivalent to £2,400 today) to watch black-and-white images on a screen less than 30 centimetres wide. Peak-time Saturday evening viewing in November 1952 was the programme *This Is Show Business*, with excerpts from classical music, ballet and opera. As a contemporary *Radio Times* informs us, 'Coco the Clown will represent the circus and Arthur Askey music hall'.

The first music series aimed at a younger audience arrived on 16 February 1957 when BBC TV launched *Six-Five Special*. Presented by actress Josephine Douglas and DJ Pete Murray, the magazine programme was introduced with the catchphrase: 'Time to jive on the old six-five.' When the BBC wanted to add educational items to the show, producer Jack Good jumped ship to ITV – a second, independent television channel that had arrived in 1955. There he launched the all-music *Oh Boy!*, which offered the whole gamut of musical styles, including jazz, rock 'n' roll and skiffle.

Going to a club meant listening to a live dance band or a small orchestra, possibly even a jazz combo for the more adventurous. If you wanted to enjoy these musicians' songs in your own home, you could consider buying the same sheet music they used. Alternatively, a selection of 12-inch 78-rpm records could be purchased from your local electrical retailer or department store to be played on a mono radiogram. As the name suggests, this was a combined radio and gramophone (or record player) and cost about 60 per cent of the average annual salary.

The launch of a 'new' weekly music paper came in 1952. The *New Musical Express*, a rebranding of the *Accordion Times and Musical Express*, was a rival to *Melody Maker* (founded in 1926), whose swathes of classified advertisements made it the go-to place if your band needed a new trombone player. Looking for a point of difference from his competitors, Percy Dickins, co-founder of the *New Musical Express*, hit upon informing readers of the discs that had been popular in shops the previous week – and so the first singles chart was born.

Prior to that, it had been simply the popularity of a song that was measured, with a chart based on sheet music sales compiled weekly by the Music Publishers Association and broadcast on Radio Luxembourg. In this chart, the sheet-music Christmas number ones were: 'Rudolph the Red-Nosed Reindeer' in 1950, with the most popular recordings by Gene Autry and Bing Crosby; and the ballad 'Longing for You' in 1951, by either American singer Teresa Brewer or our very own Teddy Johnson.

On 1 October 1954, the Official Chart expanded to a top twenty. Coincidentally, this occurred the same week as the Crew Cuts' 'Sh-Boom' entered at number sixteen – possibly the first stirrings of new-fangled rock 'n' roll music. In the middle of the decade, the BBC Light Programme introduced *Pick of the Pops* (still going on Radio 2), which played a selection of the most popular releases, but didn't introduce its own chart until 1958.

This was around the same time as the introduction of the smaller, lighter 7-inch 45-rpm record, plus something new to play it on. Step forward the Dansette, a cheaper, British-made, portable record player, perfect for the emerging teenage market to spin Bill Haley & His Comets' 'Rock Around the Clock' – the first single to become a UK million-seller.

At the beginning of 1956, Lonnie Donegan launched the skiffle boom with his single 'Rock Island Line' – a do-it-yourself blend of folk, jazz and rock 'n' roll that would inspire a generation of budding British pop stars. Buying music was now so popular that April 1956 saw the Official Chart expanded to a top thirty, with 21-year-old Elvis Presley making his debut with 'Heartbreak Hotel' the following month. In July, another new music publication, *Record Mirror*, announced the first album chart – a top-five listing with Frank Sinatra's *Songs for Swingin' Lovers!* entering at number one.

The start of 1957 saw Tommy Steele, Britain's first rock 'n' roll star, top the Official Singles Chart with 'Singing the Blues'. Before the year was out, Paul McCartney and John Lennon had become acquainted at the St Peter's Church garden fête where John's skiffle group, the Quarrymen, were playing.

In 1958, the first children of the baby boom became teenagers, with record labels, film studios and television stations all responding accordingly, albeit slowly. Surely the charts would be filled with crash-bang-wallop rock 'n' roll from now on and every Christmas number one would be a beat, pop or skiffle classic?

Let's find out…

Official Christmas Number 1

1952

AL MARTINO 'HERE IN MY HEART'

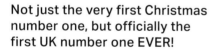

FOLLOW-UP SINGLE: 'TAKE MY HEART'
NOVEMBER 1952

WEEKS AT NUMBER ONE
9

HIGHEST CHART POSITION
9

Not just the very first Christmas number one, but officially the first UK number one EVER!

Released on a 10-inch 78-rpm (revolutions per minute) shellac disc in August 1952, Al's single was in the right places at the right time when Percy Dickins, of the *New Musical Express* (itself just nine months old), chose to ring twenty record shops and compile a list of the week's best-selling titles. And so, on 14 November 1952, the 25-year-old American singer, born Jasper Cini, found himself leading a rather curious fifteen-song 'top twelve' chart – or 'hit parade' – with three pairs of songs tying for the seventh, eighth and eleventh positions.

'Here in My Heart' remained at the top of the Official Chart for nine weeks, a benchmark that would last a full twenty months – until Yorkshire

16 January: Sooty's first TV appearance | 4 June: Songwriter and guitarist Jim Lea of Slade born |

lad David Whitfield set a new record of ten weeks with 'Cara Mia'. (More on him later...)

Although Al's follow-up single would chart for only one week, his success and Italian heritage attracted the unwanted attention of the Mafia, who bought out his management contract, thereby forcing him to flee to the UK. In 1972, life and art crossed paths when Al was cast in the role of crooner Johnny Fontaine in the film *The Godfather*.

NUMBER TWO
JO STAFFORD
'YOU BELONG TO ME'

Another American and another member of the 'inaugural chart club', Jo spent nine non-consecutive weeks at number two with 'You Belong to Me', broken up by one week in January 1953 when she supplanted Al Martino to become the first female chart-topper. Al and Jo boast the distinction of their singles having been number-one hits on both sides of the Atlantic and Jo also secured three stars on the Hollywood Walk of Fame – for her music, radio and TV work respectively.

Like Al, Jo had a second Official Chart entry before 1952 was through when her version of the

1952
CHRISTMAS TOP TEN

1 Al Martino
'Here in My Heart'

2 Jo Stafford
'You Belong to Me'

=3 Bing Crosby
'The Isle of Innisfree'

=3 Kay Starr
'Comes A-Long A-Love'

5 Guy Mitchell
'Feet Up (Pat Him on the Po-Po)'

6 Rosemary Clooney
'Half as Much'

=7 Nat 'King' Cole
'Somewhere Along the Way'

=7 Mantovani and His Orchestra
'White Christmas'

=7 Nat 'King' Cole
'Because You're Mine'

10 Johnnie Ray and the Four Lads
'Faith Can Move Mountains'

Hank Williams song 'Jambalaya' – a top-forty hit for the Carpenters in 1974 – spent two weeks at number eleven.

1953

FRANKIE LAINE
'ANSWER ME'

WEEKS AT NUMBER ONE
8

FOLLOW-UP SINGLE: 'BLOWING WILD'
JANUARY 1954

HIGHEST CHART POSITION
2

A week before the Christmas chart, Frankie Laine and David Whitfield were sharing the number-one position, each with a version of 'Answer Me'. By Christmas week itself, David had slipped to number two and Frankie was officially Christmas number one. This was Frankie's third chart-topper in an extraordinary year that saw him spend more than six months at the summit, including a record-setting eighteen non-consecutive

weeks for 'I Believe' – another song that David Whitfield released as a single and later a hit for Robson & Jerome, whose version became the duo's second number one in 1995. Frankie has the honour of being the first British artist to claim a Christmas number one – perhaps not the most impressive statistic until you consider the fact that the first six Official Chart number ones were all by American acts. We had to wait for the Stargazers, a vocal quintet, to buck the trend in April 1953 with 'Broken Wings'.

While Frankie's is the only name listed on the Official Chart itself, the single label (in a time before picture

13 April: First James Bond book, *Casino Royale*, is published | 15 May: Songwriter and guitarist

sleeves) includes credits for 'Paul Weston and His Orchestra' (Paul being the husband of Christmas number two Jo Stafford, if you were paying attention in 1952), with the Norman Luboff Choir and piano from Carl Fischer. The label also includes the subtitle 'Mütterlien', which was the song's original German title before it was given new English lyrics by Carl Sigman – the man behind Andy Williams' 1971 number four 'Where Do I Begin?', the theme from the film *Love Story*.

In an era before streaming, Frankie held the record for the most simultaneous top-ten hits when, for three weeks in 1953, 'Hey Joe', 'Answer Me', 'Where the Winds Blow' and 'I Believe' all occupied places in the upper reaches of the Official Chart.

NUMBER TWO
DAVID WHITFIELD
'ANSWER ME'

The 1953 Christmas top ten has a rather curious look to it, featuring competing versions of 'I Saw Mommy Kissing Santa Claus' and 'Swedish Rhapsody', as well as two 'Answer Me's. Though it did not make Christmas number one, David's 'Answer Me' had topped the Official Chart for one week in the first half of November. However, both David and Frankie's versions were outsold in

1953
CHRISTMAS TOP TEN

1. Frankie Laine
'Answer Me'

2. David Whitfield
'Answer Me'

3. Winifred Atwell
'Let's Have a Party'

4. Ray Martin
'Swedish Rhapsody'

5. Mantovani and His Orchestra
'Swedish Rhapsody'

6. Eddie Calvert
'Oh, Mein Papa'

7. Beverley Sisters
'I Saw Mommy Kissing Santa Claus'

8. Jimmy Boyd
'I Saw Mommy Kissing Santa Claus'

9. Guy Mitchell
'Chicka Boom'

10. Lee Lawrence
'Crying in the Chapel'

the US by Nat 'King' Cole, who took his rendition to number six in 1954. That same year, David's second number one, 'Cara Mia', became the first record by a British male singer to sell a million copies in the US and consequently the first to be awarded a gold disc. A statue celebrating the life and career of Hull-born David was unveiled outside the city's New Theatre in 2012.

Mike Oldfield born | 18 July: Sci-fi series *The Quatermass Experiment* begins on BBC TV

1954

WINIFRED ATWELL
'LET'S HAVE ANOTHER PARTY'

FOLLOW-UP SINGLE: 'LET'S HAVE A DING DONG'
NOVEMBER 1955

WEEKS AT NUMBER ONE
5

HIGHEST CHART POSITION
3

It may not surprise you to learn that 'Let's Have Another Party' is the follow-up to Winifred's 1953 number two, 'Let's Have a Party', which saw the Trinidadian pianist become the first black artist to have a number-one single in the UK and the only female artist to have a number-one instrumental single. To date, 'Let's Have Another Party' is the only instrumental Christmas number one.

The record label credits Winifred Atwell and her 'other piano', as she was known for appearing on stage with both a pristine grand and a 'worse-for-wear', slightly detuned upright – the latter reportedly bought in a Battersea junk shop for two pounds and ten shillings.

'Lucky' as well as 'other' perhaps, it was also the instrument of choice on Winifred's second number one,

6 May: Roger Bannister becomes the first runner to break the four-minute mile | 10 July: Neil Tennant

'The Poor People of Paris', which spent three weeks at the top in April 1956.

Pay attention at the back, as there will be a test on this later – 'Let's Have Another Party' is a medley of: 'Somebody Stole My Gal'; 'I Wonder Where My Baby is Tonight'; 'When the Red, Red Robin'; 'Bye Bye Blackbird'; 'The Sheik of Araby'; 'Another Little Drink'; 'Lily of Laguna'; 'Honeysuckle and the Bee'; 'Broken Doll'; 'Nellie Dean'. Keen fans of the Fab Four will know that the Beatles recorded 'The Sheik of Araby' at their unsuccessful 1962 audition for Decca Records.

Winifred's 'signature' tune, 'Black and White Rag', had a resurgence in popularity in the 1970s when it was used as the theme to the BBC snooker programme *Pot Black*.

NUMBER TWO
DAVID WHITFIELD
'SANTO NATALE'

Once again, we delve into the label credits to tell you that listed alongside David is Stanley Black and His Orchestra – composer of the theme tune to long-running radio comedy *The Goons* – and that the song is subtitled '(Happy Christmas)'. In the run-up to Christmas 2004, the record briefly slipped back into the lower end

1954
CHRISTMAS TOP TEN

1 Winifred Atwell
'Let's Have Another Party'

2 David Whitfield
'Santo Natale'

3 Ronnie Hilton
'I Still Believe'

4 Rosemary Clooney
'This Ole House'

5 Billy Eckstine
'No One But You'

6 Big Ben Banjo Band
'Let's Get Together No. 1'

7 Dickie Valentine with the Stargazers
'The Finger of Suspicion'

8 Vera Lynn
'My Son, My Son'

9 Frankie Laine and the Four Lads
'Rain, Rain, Rain'

10 Ruby Murray
'Heartbeat'

of the Official Chart based on CD single sales, spending one week at number ninety-three. The 2009 *X Factor* winner Joe McElderry recorded a version of 'Santo Natale' for his 2011 *Classic Christmas* album.

Official Christmas Number 1

1955

DICKIE VALENTINE 'CHRISTMAS ALPHABET'

FOLLOW-UP SINGLE: 'THE OLD PIANNA RAG'
DECEMBER 1955

WEEKS AT NUMBER ONE 3

HIGHEST CHART POSITION 15

This was the first of fourteen top-forty hits between 1953 and 1959, including two number ones, for the singer born Richard Bryce, but also the first of seven festive chart-toppers to date to include the word 'Christmas' in the title (or 'Xmas' in the case of Slade).

'Christmas Alphabet' was first recorded by American trio the McGuire Sisters the previous year. It was co-written by Buddy Kaye, who knew his way around an alphabet song, having written '"A" You're Adorable', a US number one for Perry Como in 1949.

At the beginning of 1955, Dickie was one of four acts to simultaneously have a version of 'Mr Sandman' in the recently enlarged top twenty.

After winning both Best British Singer and Best Vocal Personality

15 January: *The Benny Hill Show* begins on BBC TV | 14 November: Lonnie Donegan releases 'Rock Island

in the *New Musical Express*'s 1955 Pop Poll, Dickie prepared to repeat his Official Chart triumph in 1956 by releasing 'Christmas Island', which peaked at number eight, as well as a back-up plan in the shape of *Dickie Valentine's Rock 'n' Roll Party* (EP), with 'Christmas Rock 'n' Roll' as its lead track.

In 1957, Dickie hired the Royal Albert Hall to accommodate fan-club members wanting to attend his annual get-together, though his festive offering for that year, 'Snowbound for Christmas', missed out on the Yuletide chart, creeping in at number twenty-eight for one week in early January 1958.

NUMBER TWO
BILL HALEY & HIS COMETS
'ROCK AROUND THE CLOCK'

The sandwich bread to the 'Christmas Alphabet' filling, 'Rock Around the Clock' spent three weeks before and two weeks after Dickie's chart-topper in the number-one slot.

The Comets' first hit, 'Shake, Rattle and Roll', had reached number four in January 1954 and 'Rock Around the Clock', their follow-up single, originally hit number seventeen in January 1955, but dropped out of the chart (at the time a top twenty) after only two weeks. It re-charted

1955
CHRISTMAS TOP TEN

1 Dickie Valentine
'Christmas Alphabet'

2 Bill Haley & His Comets
'Rock Around the Clock'

3 Max Bygraves
'Meet Me on the Corner'

4 Winifred Atwell
'Let's Have a Ding Dong'

5 Four Aces feat. Al Alberts
'Love Is a Many-Splendored Thing'

6 The Stargazers
'Twenty Tiny Fingers'

7 Frankie Laine
'Hawk-Eye'

8 Petula Clark
'Suddenly There's a Valley'

9 Johnston Brothers and the George Chilsholm Sour-Note Six
'Join In and Sing Again'

10 Alma Cogan
'Never Do a Tango with an Eskimo'

in October after its inclusion in the film *Blackboard Jungle*. Following another eighteen weeks in the Official Chart in 1956, it became the first UK million-selling single and would chart again in 1968 and 1974.

THE ORIGINAL POP IDOLS

The phrase 'before Elvis, there was nothing' may have rung true for John Lennon (to whom it is attributed), but the Official Chart would suggest otherwise. Here we take a longing look at a handful of the pre-Presley crooners, dreamboats and heartthrobs who knew their way around a holiday hit…

Frank Sinatra
Where else to start than with Ol' Blue Eyes, the Italian-American crooner who began his recording career fronting the Harry James Orchestra? With a reported 1,000 fan clubs across the US, Frank topped *Billboard* and *DownBeat* magazines' 'best male singer' polls in the 1940s, while his appearance at the New York Paramount Theatre in October 1944 was dubbed the 'Columbus Day Riot' after 30,000 screaming fans gathered in Times Square.

His early festive output includes a version of 'White Christmas' in 1944, 'Jingle Bells' in 1946 and the album *Christmas Songs by Sinatra* in 1948. He made his UK Official Chart debut with the 1954 number twelve 'Young at Heart' and had his first number one the same year when 'Three Coins in the Fountain' spent three weeks at the top. However, it wasn't until the age of streaming that Frank's seasonal output crept into the lower reaches of the Official Chart; his 1950 recording of 'Let It Snow! Let It Snow! Let It Snow!' peaked at number fifty-six in 2020.

Doris Day
The Golden Globe- and Grammy Award-winning actress and singer born Doris Kappelhoff first found mainstream Stateside success in 1945 with the song 'Sentimental Journey'. After appearing in our first ever Official Chart with 'Sugarbush', a duet with Frankie Laine (our 1953 Christmas number-one artist), Doris had her second hit the following week with 'My Love and Devotion'. This was the second of her fifteen top-forty hits, which would include the number ones 'Secret Love' (nine weeks at the top in 1954) and 'Whatever Will Be, Will Be (Que Sera Sera)' (six weeks in 1956).

Among Doris's early festive frolics was a 1947 recording of 'The Christmas Song' (the song that starts with 'chestnuts roasting on an open fire'), which eventually made the Official Chart in 1990 when it reached number eighty-seven. Comedienne Tracey Ullman's cover of 'Move Over Darling' – originally a 1964 number eight for Doris – just missed out on a place in our 1983 Christmas top ten when it dropped from number nine to number twelve on Christmas Eve.

Perry Como
We have to go back to 1936 for the recording debut of Pierino 'Perry' Como and the song 'You Can't Pull the Wool Over My Eyes'. In an era when the measure of popularity included radio plays and jukebox selection, Perry had a hit with a 1946 recording of 'Winter Wonderland' – one of eight songs included on his album the following year, *Perry Como Sings Merry Christmas Music*.

In February 1953, Perry became just the fifth artist to have a number-one single in the nascent Official Chart when 'Don't Let the Stars Get in Your Eyes' began a five-week run at the top. It was the first of twenty-six top-forty hits for Perry, which would include a second number one in 1958 with 'Magic Moments' and a number-seven spot in our Christmas top ten that same year. (Some readers and aficionados of TV adverts may experience an urge to buy a tin of Quality Street chocolates at the mention of 'Magic Moments'.) Perry's 1951 recording of 'It's Beginning to Look a Lot Like Christmas' is another Official Chart repeat returnee, peaking at number forty-seven in 2008.

Rosemary Clooney

The Christmas credentials of singer and actress Rosemary Clooney would already be beyond doubt if we only mentioned her role as Betty Haynes in the 1954 film *White Christmas*, in which she starred alongside Bing Crosby, Danny Kaye and Vera-Ellen. Rosemary made her recording debut in 1948 (fronting Tony Pastor's orchestra) with 'You Started Something' and then had a big US hit in 1951 with 'Come On-a My House'. Meanwhile, her Yuletide offerings included 'Let's Give a Present to Santa Claus' and 'He'll Be Coming Down the Chimney'.

Like Doris Day, Rosemary's Official Chart debut was in that very first 1952 listing. The single, 'Half as Much', was the first of seven top-forty hits for Rosemary, which would include the number ones 'This Ole House' (one week in December 1954, although skip to Christmas 1985 for more on this song) and 'Mambo Italiano' (three weeks in early 1955), which was also a top-twenty hit for Dean Martin. Speaking of whom…

Dean Martin

Born Dino Crocetti and reportedly called the 'King of Cool' by Elvis, Dean embraced the Yuletide spirit with recordings of 'Baby, It's Cold Outside' (later reworked as a posthumous duet with country singer Martina McBride) and 'Rudolph the Red-Nosed Reindeer'. In October 1953, he made his Official Chart debut with the number-five single 'Kiss' – the first

of seventeen top-forty hits, which would include the 1954 number one 'Memories Are Made of This'. Dean died on Christmas Day in 1995.

Like Frank Sinatra, Dean was associated with the American entertainers dubbed the 'Rat Pack' and both singers appeared in the 1960 film *Ocean's 11*. (Incidentally, the film was remade in 2001 with Rosemary Clooney's nephew George taking the title role.) Also, like Frank, Dean's version of 'Let It Snow! Let It Snow! Let It Snow!' – included on his 1959 album, *A Winter Romance* – is a regular visitor to the December charts, peaking at number thirty-seven at the end of 2020.

Ruby Murray

From closer to home comes Belfast-born Ruby Murray, whose roots are made obvious by her choice of festive repertoire, including the songs 'Christmas in Ireland' and 'Christmas in Killarney' – both taken from her album *Irish … And Proud of It*. Ruby made her Official Chart debut with 'Heartbeat', which brought up the rear of our 1954 Christmas top ten and reached a number-three peak the following February. It was the first of ten top-forty hits for Ruby, which would include the 1955 number one 'Softly Softly'.

In the last week of March that year, Ruby had five songs in the top twenty: 'Softly Softly' was number two; 'Let Me Go Lover' was number six; 'If Anyone Finds This, I Love You' (a duet with Anne Warren) was at number ten; her version of that now-familiar favourite 'Mambo Italiano' was at number sixteen; and 'Happy Days and Lonely Nights' sat at number nineteen. A melody from Ruby's 1958 recording 'Believe Me, If All Those Endearing Young Charms' was interpolated in the introduction of Dexys Midnight Runners' 1982 UK and US number one, 'Come On Eileen'.

Official Christmas Number 1

1956

JOHNNIE RAY 'JUST WALKING IN THE RAIN'

FOLLOW-UP SINGLE: 'LOOK HOMEWARD, ANGEL'
JANUARY 1957

WEEKS AT NUMBER ONE
7

HIGHEST CHART POSITION
7

This was the second of three number-one hits for the singer once described by Tony Bennett as the 'father of rock and roll'. Perhaps less kindly, the media dubbed Johnnie 'The Prince of Wails' and 'The Nabob of Sob' in response to his emotional stage act and his 1951 US number ones 'Cry' and 'The Little White Cloud that Cried'.

The original song, 'Just Walkin' in the Rain', was written in 1952 by Johnny Bragg and Robert Riley, inmates of Tennessee Prison, and was first recorded by the Prisonaires, Bragg's doo-wop group, for Sam Phillips' Sun Records the following year.

Partially deafened as a child, Johnnie wore a hearing aid from the age of fourteen, supposedly the inspiration behind Morrissey wearing one for a 1984 *Top of the Pops* appearance. Johnnie had his first UK chart-topper in April 1954 – a cover of US soul group the Drifters' 'Such a Night' – and his third in May 1957 with single 'Yes

31 January: John Lydon (aka Johnny Rotten) born | 24 May: Inaugural Eurovision Song Contest is

Tonight Josephine', which returned to the chart in 1981 at number twenty-five, thanks to rockabilly revival band the Jets.

In 1969, Johnnie was best man at Judy Garland's fifth and final wedding to nightclub pianist Mickey Deans. He also made a return (of sorts) to the Official Chart in 1982 when Dexys Midnight Runners namechecked him in their number-one hit 'Come On Eileen' and used footage of him arriving at Heathrow Airport in the promo video.

NUMBER TWO
GUY MITCHELL
'SINGING THE BLUES'

The third of four UK number-one singles for the American singer born Albert Cernik, 'Singing the Blues' spent ten weeks at number one on the US *Billboard* chart, but had to settle for three separate weeks in the UK, trading the top spot with a rival version of the song by homegrown talent Tommy Steele.

Those three spells at the top put Guy in elite company. Other artists to have topped the Official Chart three times with the same song are: former Christmas number-one title-holder Frankie Laine (with 'I Believe'); Baddiel, Skinner and the Lightning Seeds (with the original version of 'Three Lions'); Pharrell

1956
CHRISTMAS TOP TEN

1 Johnnie Ray
'Just Walking in the Rain'

2 Guy Mitchell
'Singing the Blues'

=3 Malcolm Vaughan
'St Therese of the Roses'

=3 Frankie Vaughan
'The Green Door'

5 Bing Crosby and Grace Kelly
'True Love'

6 Eddie Fisher
'Cindy, Oh Cindy'

7 Winifred Atwell
'Make It a Party'

8 Dickie Valentine
'Christmas Island'

9 Bill Haley & His Comets
'Rip It Up'

10 The Platters
'My Prayer'

Williams (with 'Happy'); Justin Bieber (with both 'What Do You Mean?' and 'Despacito (Remix)') and the Weeknd (with 'Blinding Lights').

Meanwhile, cover versions of 'Singing the Blues' have been top-forty hits for two later Christmas number-one artists: Dave Edmunds in 1980 (whose cover reached number twenty-eight); and Cliff Richard and the Shadows in 2009 (who edged in at number forty).

Official Christmas Number 1

1957

HARRY BELAFONTE
'MARY'S BOY CHILD'

FOLLOW-UP SINGLE: 'LITTLE BERNADETTE'
AUGUST 1958

WEEKS AT NUMBER ONE
7

HIGHEST CHART POSITION
16

The New Yorker born Harold Bellanfanti Jr had begun singing pop and jazz standards to pay for acting classes, but an interest in folk music culminated in his 1956 album *Calypso* staying at the top of the US album chart for thirty-one weeks. 'Mary's Boy Child' capped a stellar 1957 for Harry, which began with his UK Official Chart debut 'The Banana Boat Song' reaching number two in April, earning him the epithet 'King of Calypso'.

He had previously recorded 'Mary's Boy Child' in December 1956 when it had reached number 12 in the US and failed to chart in the UK. His new, longer version finally topped the UK Official Chart at the end of November 1957 when it replaced 'That'll Be the Day' by the Crickets at number one.

To encourage radio play (particularly in the US), singles were typically no longer than three minutes, allowing

16 January: The Cavern Club opens in Liverpool | 24 April: Patrick Moore presents the first episode

time for commercials and witty DJ banter. And so, at four minutes and twelve seconds long, 'Mary's Boy Child' became the UK number-one single with the longest runtime, though it also achieved a less impressive feat in January 1958 when it became the first song to drop from number one straight out of the top ten. The following two Christmases saw its return to the Official Chart when it reached number ten in 1958 and number thirty in 1959. (It will also be a hot topic once more when we come to discuss Christmas 1978…)

NUMBER TWO
JOHNNY OTIS AND HIS ORCHESTRA WITH MARIE ADAMS AND THE THREE TONS OF JOY
'MA (HE'S MAKING EYES AT ME)'

The first of just two chart entries for Johnny Otis, this single includes a label credit for singer Marie Adams and the 'Three Tons of Joy' – an uncomplimentary reference to her sisters Sadie and Francine McKinley.

In 1974, a version by ten-year-old Scottish singer Lena Zavaroni reached number ten. Her album of the same name also made her the youngest person to have a top-ten album. Johnny Otis had his only

1957
CHRISTMAS TOP TEN

1. **Harry Belafonte**
'Mary's Boy Child'

2. **Johnny Otis and His Orchestra with Marie Adams and the Three Tons of Joy**
'Ma (He's Making Eyes at Me)'

3. **Malcolm Vaughan**
'My Special Angel'

4. **Winifred Atwell**
'Let's Have a Ball'

5. **Frank Sinatra**
'All the Way'

6. **Jerry Lee Lewis**
'Great Balls of Fire'

7. **Everly Brothers**
'Wake Up Little Susie'

8. **Paul Anka**
'I Love You Baby'

9. **Petula Clark**
'Alone'

10. **Jackie Wilson**
'Reet Petite (The Sweetest Girl in Town'

other hit with the 1958 number twenty 'Bye Bye Baby', though a co-writing credit for the Elvis Presley single 'Hound Dog' must have sweetened the blow.

Also in 1957's top ten is a title that will bide its time for almost three decades before becoming a surprise Christmas number one in 1986…

1958

CONWAY TWITTY 'IT'S ONLY MAKE BELIEVE'

FOLLOW-UP SINGLE: 'THE STORY OF MY LOVE'
MARCH 1959

WEEKS AT NUMBER ONE
5

HIGHEST CHART POSITION
30

Originally released as the B-side of his US single 'I'll Try', 'It's Only Make Believe' has the distinction of being the first self-penned Christmas number one – it was written by Conway with his drummer Jack Nance. It was his Official Chart debut and the biggest of four top-forty hits, including a number-five cover of 'Mona Lisa', more readily associated with Nat 'King' Cole.

It is also the (Christmas) gift that keeps on giving, as Billy Fury, Glen Campbell and British pop quartet Child all took their own versions into the top ten in subsequent decades. A further murmur of appreciation for Billy, who spent 231 weeks in the top forty without ever having a number one.

31 August: The first Carry On film, *Carry On Sergeant*, is released | **10 September:** Siobhan Fahey of

Conway also recorded a new version in 1970 as a duet with country music superstar Loretta Lynn.

Born Harold Lloyd Jenkins in 1933, he reportedly chose his stage name from a road map showing Conway in Arkansas and Twitty in Texas. In 1970, he launched his own Twitty Burgers restaurant in Oklahoma City – among its opening-night guests was Dolly Parton – and he also opened a theatre in 1982, adjacent to his home in Hendersonville, Tennessee, which he named Twitty City.

By way of reference, Peter Sellers – who went on to have a top-ten hit in December 1960 with 'Goodness Gracious Me', a duet with actress Sophia Loren – used the name 'Twit Conway' for a sketch on his 1959 album *Songs for Swingin' Sellers*. The line-up included other fictitious pop acts such as Lenny Bronze, Clint Thigh and Matt Lust.

NUMBER TWO
LORD ROCKINGHAM'S XI
'HOOTS MON'

The first of two top-forty hits for a group of musicians led by Harry Robinson. Lord Rockingham's XI was assembled to act as the house band on the ITV programme *Oh Boy!* – the first all-music show aimed at teenagers, which ran between

1958
CHRISTMAS TOP TEN

1 **Conway Twitty**
'It's Only Make Believe'

2 **Lord Rockingham's XI**
'Hoots Mon'

3 **Lonnie Donegan**
'Tom Dooley'

=4 **Tommy Edwards**
'It's All in the Game'

=4 **Tommy Dorsey Orchestra starring Warren Covington**
'Tea for Two Cha Cha'

6 **Kingston Trio**
'Tom Dooley'

7 **Perry Como**
'Love Makes the World Go 'Round'

8 **Jane Morgan**
'The Day the Rains Came'

9 **Cliff Richard and the Drifters**
'High Class Baby'

10 **Tommy Steele**
'Come On, Let's Go'

1958 and 1959. 'Hoots Mon' – a rock 'n' roll version of the traditional Scottish song 'A Hundred Pipers' – spent three weeks at number one, displacing Tommy Edwards' ballad 'It's All in the Game', but lost out to Conway Twitty just before Christmas. Harry Robinson later wrote the string arrangements for folk singer Nick Drake's melancholy masterpiece 'River Man'.

1959

EMILE FORD AND THE CHECKMATES
'WHAT DO YOU WANT TO MAKE THOSE EYES AT ME FOR?'

FOLLOW-UP SINGLE: 'A SLOW BOAT TO CHINA'
FEBRUARY 1960

WEEKS AT NUMBER ONE
6

HIGHEST CHART POSITION
3

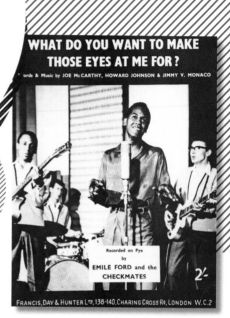

WHAT DO YOU WANT TO MAKE THOSE EYES AT ME FOR?

Words & Music by JOE McCARTHY, HOWARD JOHNSON & JIMMY V. MONACO

Recorded on Pye
by
EMILE FORD and the CHECKMATES

2/-

FRANCIS, DAY & HUNTER L.TD, 138-140, CHARING CROSS RR, LONDON W.C.2

In early 1959, the Checkmates, fronted by Saint Lucia-born Emile Ford, won the Best Vocal Group contest staged by *Disc* magazine as part of the Soho Fair event in London, resulting in a record deal with Pye Records. Their debut single was a version of 'Don't Tell Me Your Troubles', a minor hit in the US for country singer Don Gibson. Hidden away on the B-side was a doo-wop arrangement of 'What Do

You Want to Make Those Eyes at Me For?', originally written for the 1916 Broadway musical *Follow Me*. It spent almost six months in the top forty, including a six-week spell at number one, until it was dethroned by Michael Holliday's 'Starry Eyed'.

The Checkmates maintained their festive output by recording a version of 'White Christmas' as the flip of their 1960 number-four single 'Counting Teardrops'. They also augmented their line-up with keyboard player Alan Hawkshaw,

1 June: *Juke Box Jury* begins on BBC TV | 24 June: Andy McCluskey (OMD) born | 26 August: The

whose credits could fill books much bigger than this, though his theme music for *Countdown* and *Grange Hill* deserve a mention.

And the song's appeal endured: Swedish group Hep Stars, featuring a young Benny Andersson of ABBA fame, recorded 'What Do You Want to Make Those Eyes at Me For?' on their 1965 album, *Hep Stars on Stage*; Mud singer Les Gray released a version as a solo single in 1977; and recurring Christmas chart favourite Shakin' Stevens took his rendition to number five in December 1987.

NUMBER TWO
ADAM FAITH
'WHAT DO YOU WANT?'

With his fourth attempt for three different labels, Adam Faith made his Official Chart debut and had the first of two number-one hits when 'What Do You Want?' spent three weeks at the top (one week shared with Emile Ford), establishing the record for the shortest chart-topper runtime, clocking in at one minute and thirty-eight seconds.

Adam can't claim the first 'question'-themed number one – that honour goes to Lita Ford for her 1953 hit '(How Much Is) That Doggie in the Window?' – but he does figure in a

1959
CHRISTMAS TOP TEN

1. **Emile Ford and the Checkmates**
'What Do You Want to Make Those Eyes at Me For?'

2. **Adam Faith**
'What Do You Want?'

3. **Neil Sedaka**
'Oh! Carol'

4. **The Avons**
'Seven Little Girls Sitting in the Back Seat'

5. **Russ Conway**
'More and More Party Pops'

6. **Elmer Bernstein**
'Staccato's Theme'

7. **Russ Conway**
'Snow Coach'

8. **Cliff Richard and the Shadows**
'Travellin' Light'

9. **Johnny and the Hurricanes**
'Red River Rock'

10. **Tommy Steele**
'Little White Bull'

rather unique chart sequence where a 'question' song at number one is replaced by another 'question' song that features the title of its predecessor in its own title.

WELCOME TO THE '60s

Little changed for music fans when the new decade dawned, with rock 'n' roll, skiffle, trad jazz, toe-tapping instrumentals and unthreatening crooners still popular. Homegrown talent began to provide some competition for the American acts, however, and change certainly was afoot in the Official Chart, which added twenty places to its weekly list of best-selling singles from March 1960. Quite appropriately, the first ever number thirty-one was 'Fings Ain't Wot They Used T'Be' by Max Bygraves.

The BBC still had a monopoly on radio broadcasting, though the demand for pop music saw listener options grow, with Radio Luxembourg joined by 'pirate' stations Radio Caroline and Radio London in 1964, both transmitting from ships in international waters. They were outlawed by the Marine Broadcasting Offences Act of 1967 and the BBC responded by replacing its existing stations with new offerings: the Light Programme was split into Radio 1 (pop and rock) and Radio 2 ('easy listening'); the Third Programme became Radio 3 (classical music); and the Home Service was renamed Radio 4 (news and spoken word).

Most broadcasts were in mono and, even though stereo records had been available since the late '50s, it wasn't until the end of the '60s that they became more commonplace. Even then, some acts would release albums in both mono and stereo, reflecting the lack of equipment to showcase the new sounds at their best.

Television recognised the opportunity music offered, if only for a couple of hours a week, and there was a steady stream of new programmes vying for viewers' attention. On ITV, *Boy Meets Girl* replaced *Oh Boy!* at the end of 1959, lasting just one series before it was itself replaced, this time by *Wham!!* (two exclamation marks), from the same producer – Jack Good – and featuring many of the same performers.

Juke Box Jury began on BBC TV in 1958 and continued until December 1967, with host David Jacobs asking a panel of guests to declare a selection of records a 'Hit' or a 'Miss'. The ITV response was *Thank Your Lucky Stars*, on which artists mimed to their latest single and a panel of judges rated the songs on a 1–5 scale. It ran for 250 episodes from April 1961 to December 1966.

The first, seemingly unremarkable, appearance of the Beatles in the Official Chart came in October 1962 when 'Love Me Do' entered at number forty-nine, sandwiched between the third of three releases by London-born actor and singer Jess Conrad and a fourteenth entry for American rocker Little Richard. 'Love Me Do' took eleven weeks to climb to a number-seventeen peak – a good but hardly auspicious start to the band's recording career. With an average age of twenty, the Beatles combined the stagecraft of more mature acts (their manager, Brian Epstein, took them out of jeans and leather jackets and into matching suits) with the rebellious streak of rockers.

However, it was the Beatles' songwriting skills that really set them apart. At the time, it was common practice for artist managers or record-company A&R (artists and repertoire) men to match performers with songwriters or publishers – the latter centred around Denmark Street in London, known as Britain's 'Tin Pan Alley'. To put it into perspective, prior to the Beatles' arrival, Cliff Richard had a co-writing credit on just one of his seven UK chart-topping songs, while Elvis Presley also had a sole credit from his total of sixteen number ones. By way of contrast, John Lennon and Paul McCartney wrote every single one of their nineteen chart-topping songs.

On a Friday evening in August 1963, music programme *Ready Steady Go!* announced itself with the tagline, 'The weekend starts here!' It attracted the biggest names of the day and helped introduce a wider UK audience to Motown artists like the Supremes and Marvin Gaye, as well as James Brown, Otis Redding and the Beach Boys. *Top of the Pops* began on 1 January 1964 and would dominate music television in the UK for the next twenty-five years, influencing and reflecting the Official Chart, with a Christmas special from the outset that would inform many memories of festive hits.

Cinema got in on the act, too, with films like the Beatles' *A Hard Day's Night*, Gerry and the Pacemakers' *Ferry Cross the Mersey* and the Dave Clark Five's *Catch Us If You Can* picking up where *The Tommy Steele Story* and the Cliff Richard feature *Expresso Bongo* left off in the previous decade. Films were also a great way of reaching overseas markets, particularly the US, where the success of the UK bands sparked the 'British Invasion', with fashion and film joining music as part of this friendly phenomenon.

It was not unusual for bands in smaller venues to play two or even three shows a day. In the larger theatres, live performances would be a revue – a continuation of the music-hall tradition – with a compère introducing as many as ten acts, each playing for no more than half an hour. The second half of the decade also saw the emergence of pop and rock music festivals, traditionally the preserve of the jazz and blues crowds. As songwriting developed and recording techniques improved, venues got bigger and more sophisticated light shows were introduced, although sound technology struggled to keep up with the pace.

In April 1966, US magazine *Time* proclaimed London 'The Swinging City'. Pop music started to look further afield for new influences, songs and hair got longer, and there was a school of thought that rock music was where it was at. That same year, the Official Albums Chart grew from a top twenty to a top forty to reflect demand for this more serious format. Surely the charts would showcase only top-to-bottom, 'turn on, tune in, drop out' music from now on and every Christmas number one would be a psychedelic, jazz-rock or folk-rock classic?

Let's find out…

Official Christmas Number 1

1960

CLIFF RICHARD AND THE SHADOWS
'I LOVE YOU'

FOLLOW-UP SINGLE: 'THEME FOR A DREAM'
MARCH 1961

WEEKS AT NUMBER ONE
2

HIGHEST CHART POSITION
3

This was the third consecutive appearance in the Christmas top ten (you'll find 'High Class Baby' at number nine in 1958 and 'Travellin' Light' at number eight in 1959) and the fourth number one for Cliff and the Shadows, though pedants may wish to point out that the Shadows were still called the Drifters when they claimed their first chart-topper, 'Living Doll'. The enforced name change was brought on by a legal notice from American vocal group the Drifters, who coincidentally occupy the number-five slot in our 1960 Christmas top ten.

Despite the seemingly obvious title for an Official Chart hit, the only other top-forty 'I Love You' is Donna Summer's 1977 number ten (with a mention in dispatches for Yello, whose own 'I Love You' stalled at number forty-one in 1983).

4 April: RCA Victor Records announces it will release all pop singles in mono and stereo simultaneously |

Cliff had his first number one in August 1959 (the aforementioned 'Living Doll') and his most recent in December 1999, with 'Millennium Prayer' – more on that song later...

This gap of forty years, four months and fifteen days is the second largest for any artist, beaten only by a certain Elvis Presley – more on him now...

NUMBER TWO
ELVIS PRESLEY
'IT'S NOW OR NEVER'

Slipping to number two after eight weeks at the top, Elvis's fifth number one had a slightly convoluted birth, with a melody derived from an 1898 Neapolitan song 'O Sole Mio', which was given English lyrics in 1949 and recorded as 'There's No Tomorrow' by American singer Tony Martin. It was this version that Private (later Sergeant) Elvis Presley – serial number: 53310761 – heard while stationed in West Germany with the US Army.

Elvis's run of chart-toppers began in June 1957 with 'All Shook Up' and continued with at least one number one in each of the following six years. 'It's Now or Never' became Elvis's twenty-first and most recent number one, too: the song's 2005 re-issue added

1960
CHRISTMAS TOP TEN

1. **Cliff Richard and the Shadows**
'I Love You'

2. **Elvis Presley**
'It's Now or Never'

3. **Anthony Newley**
'Strawberry Fair'

4. **Nina & Frederik**
'Little Donkey'

5. **The Drifters**
'Save the Last Dance for Me'

6. **Johnny Tillotson**
'Poetry in Motion'

7. **Adam Faith**
'Lonely Pup (In a Christmas Shop)'

8. **Johnny and the Hurricanes**
'Rocking Goose'

9. **The Shadows**
'Man of Mystery'/'The Stranger'

10. **Connie Francis**
'My Heart Has a Mind of Its Own'

one more chart-topping week to Elvis's eighty-week total – the most for any artist. 'All Shook Up' and 'It's Now or Never' also set the record for the longest span between any artist's first and last number one, with forty-seven years, six months and twenty-three days separating the two hits.

1961
DANNY WILLIAMS
'MOON RIVER'

WEEKS AT NUMBER ONE
2

FOLLOW-UP SINGLE: 'JEANNIE'
JANUARY 1962

HIGHEST CHART POSITION
14

After two singles that stalled just outside of the top forty ('The Miracle of You' spent three consecutive weeks at number forty-one in July 1961), South African-born Danny had the first of his five hits with the ballad 'Moon River'.

Composed by Henry Mancini and Johnny Mercer (a version by the former briefly appeared at number forty-four when Danny's went to number one), 'Moon River' was first performed by Audrey Hepburn in the 1961 film *Breakfast at Tiffany's*. While that version won an Oscar and two Grammy Awards, the song is perhaps more readily associated with another Williams, Andy, though his version was never released as a single in the UK.

In 1963, 'Williams, D.' joined a twenty-city UK tour headlined by

3 April: The 150-mph Jaguar E-Type sports car launched | 17 October: Mick Jagger meets Keith

Helen Shapiro, with a promising new turn called the Beatles listed fourth on the eleven-act bill.

After his fourth hit (the 1962 number twenty-two 'Tears'), Danny had to wait fifteen years for his final visit to the top forty, courtesy of the disco-flavoured 'Dancin' Easy'. The single reached number thirty in August 1977 and featured a co-writing credit for DJ Chris Hill, whose comedy records 'Renta Santa' and 'Bionic Santa' can be seen in our 1975 and 1976 Christmas top tens, respectively.

NUMBER TWO
FRANKIE VAUGHAN
'TOWER OF STRENGTH'

This was Frankie's second number one in a chart career that spanned fifteen years and twenty-nine top-forty hits, though curiously didn't include his signature tune, 'Give Me the Moonlight'. Having entered the Official Chart in mid-November, 'Tower of Strength' reached number one a month later, ending Elvis Presley's four-week stay at the top with 'His Latest Flame'.

The song – with music by Burt Bacharach and words by Bob Hilliard (the latter also responsible for the Avons' 'Seven Little Girls Sitting in the Back Seat') – was originally recorded by Gene McDaniels. His

1961
CHRISTMAS TOP TEN

1. **Danny Williams**
'Moon River'

2. **Frankie Vaughan**
'Tower of Strength'

3. **Kenny Ball and His Jazzmen**
'Midnight in Moscow'

4. **Sandy Nelson**
'Let There Be Drums'

5. **Pat Boone**
'Johnny Will'

6. **Acker Bilk**
'Stranger on the Shore'

7. **Russ Conway**
'Toy Balloons'

8. **Bobby Vee**
'Take Good Care of My Baby'

9. **Petula Clark**
'My Friend the Sea'

10. **Neil Sedaka**
'Happy Birthday, Sweet Sixteen'

version reached number five in the US, but only peaked at number forty-nine in the UK.

Frankie made his film debut in the 1956 comedy western *Ramsbottom Rides Again*, starring Arthur Askey. His cinematic career then got a little more glamourous when he appeared opposite Marilyn Monroe in the 1960 Hollywood musical *Let's Make Love*.

Official
Christmas
Number 1

1962

ELVIS PRESLEY
'RETURN TO SENDER'

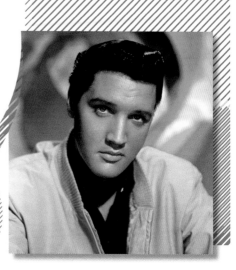

FOLLOW-UP SINGLE: 'ONE BROKEN HEART FOR SALE'
FEBRUARY 1963

WEEKS AT NUMBER ONE
3

HIGHEST CHART POSITION
12

'Telstar' by the Tornados became only the second British recording to top the US chart (the first did so earlier in 1962 and was also an instrumental – 'Stranger on the Shore' by Acker Bilk).

Elvis's thirteenth number-one single was written for his 1962 film *Girls! Girls! Girls!* and can boast the honour of being the first Christmas number one in Ireland (the Official Irish Singles Chart was launched in October that year).

In the US, 'Return to Sender' spent five weeks at number two, kept from the top by the Four Seasons' 'Big Girls Don't Cry'. By Christmas week, it had slipped to number six when

Meanwhile, back in the UK, Elvis's total of 1,060 weeks in the top forty now includes the longest continuous run by any artist – 135 weeks between July 1960 (when 'A Mess of Blues' first charted) and February 1963 (when 'Return to Sender' left the chart) – and encompasses twelve different hits, among them nine number ones.

Luckily for us, Elvis is a veritable treasure trove of pop stats, including

17 March: Clare Grogan of Altered Images born | 14 June: *Steptoe and Son* begins on BBC TV | 28 August:

the Official Chart double: holding both the number-one album and single slot in the same week. The first artist to achieve this (with the album *G.I. Blues* and the single 'Are You Lonesome Tonight?' in 1961), Elvis repeated the feat in 1962 when *Blue Hawaii* topped the Official Albums Chart while 'Rock-A-Hula Baby', 'Can't Help Falling in Love' and 'Good Luck Charm' all became number-one singles. And there's more – Elvis has peaked at number two a record seventeen times, though eight of those were with posthumous re-issues of tracks that had previously reached number one.

NUMBER TWO
CLIFF RICHARD AND THE SHADOWS
'THE NEXT TIME'/ 'BACHELOR BOY'

We almost had a repeat of our 1960 top two, but this time Elvis held on for an extra week to secure what would be his only Christmas number one. Cliff's double A-side release would still reach the summit in the first chart of 1963 – becoming his sixth number one – and both sides of the single were taken from his very own 1962 celluloid vehicle, *Summer Holiday*.

'The Next Time' features a credit for the Norrie Paramor Strings, while

1962
CHRISTMAS TOP TEN

1. **Elvis Presley**
'Return to Sender'

2. **Cliff Richard and the Shadows**
'The Next Time'/'Bachelor Boy'

3. **The Shadows**
'Dance On!'

4. **Duane Eddy**
'(Dance with the) Guitar Man'

5. **Frank Ifield**
'Lovesick Blues'

6. **Brenda Lee**
'Rockin' Around the Christmas Tree'

7. **Rolf Harris**
'Sun Arise'

8. **The Tornados**
'Telstar'

9. **Susan Maughan**
'Bobby's Girl'

10. **Chris Montez**
'Let's Dance'

'Bachelor Boy' is actually the first of Cliff's chart-toppers to feature a co-writing credit for Cliff himself, shared with Shadows guitarist Bruce Welch.

Elsewhere in the 1962 top ten, the Shadows can be found at number three with the instrumental single 'Dance On!', ready to replace themselves (and Cliff) at number one three weeks later.

BBC radio begins experimental stereo broadcasts | October: Premiere of first James Bond film, *Dr No*

Official Christmas Number 1

1963

THE BEATLES
'I WANT TO HOLD YOUR HAND'

WEEKS AT NUMBER ONE
5

FOLLOW-UP SINGLE: 'CAN'T BUY ME LOVE'
MARCH 1964

HIGHEST CHART POSITION
1

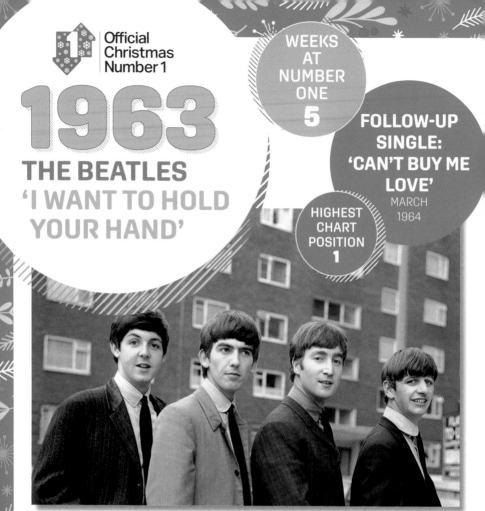

When 'I Want to Hold Your Hand' overtook 'She Loves You' at the top on 12 December 1963 it was, strictly speaking, the first time an artist replaced themselves at number one, though the Shadows had already replaced Cliff Richard and the Shadows (and vice versa). Both 'I Want to Hold Your Hand' and its B-side, 'This Boy', were recorded on 17 October 1963 – a good day's work for a record that sold more than 13 million copies worldwide.

In France the following January, the Beatles re-recorded 'I Want to Hold Your Hand' and 'She Loves You' in German, with 'Komm, gib mir deine Hand' and 'Sie liebt dich' reaching

25 June: Singer and songwriter George Michael born | 9 August: *Ready Steady Go!* begins on ITV |

number one and number seven on the German charts, respectively.

On that same productive October day, the Beatles also recorded the first of seven annual Christmas records sent out to members of their fan club. It included a rendition of the carol 'Good King Wenceslas', messages from each band member (scripted by their press officer, Tony Barrow) and a chorus of 'Rudolph the Red-Nosed Ringo'. They had originally planned to send out 25,000 copies, but eventually posted 31,000 due to additional demand; even then, Bettina Rose and Anne Collingham – joint national secretaries of the fan club – had to send a letter of apology to unlucky fans whose membership application forms and five-shilling postal orders arrived too late.

NUMBER TWO
THE BEATLES
'SHE LOVES YOU'

The Beatles claimed their second number one of 1963 on 12 September ('From Me to You' had spent seven consecutive weeks at the top, beginning in early May). This was followed by a run of seven weeks of 'She Loves You' sitting at either number two or three, before returning to the top for two more weeks on 28 November.

1963
CHRISTMAS TOP TEN

1. **The Beatles**
'I Want to Hold Your Hand'

2. **The Beatles**
'She Loves You'

3. **Freddie and the Dreamers**
'You Were Made for Me'

4. **Kathy Kirby**
'Secret Love'

5. **Dusty Springfield**
'I Only Want to Be with You'

6. **Dave Clark Five**
'Glad All Over'

7. **Singing Nun**
'Dominique'

8. **Cliff Richard and the Shadows**
'Don't Talk to Him'

9. **Gene Pitney**
'Twenty-Four Hours from Tulsa'

10. **Los Indios Tabajaras**
'Maria Elena'

'She Loves You' was one of four songs the Beatles performed at the Royal Command Performance on 4 November. Upon being presented to the Queen Mother, the band members were asked where their next performance would be. The answer was Slough, to which the Queen Mother remarked, 'Oh, that's near us.' Slough is a couple of miles from Windsor Castle.

22 November: US president John F. Kennedy assassinated | 23 November: *Doctor Who* begins on BBC TV

1964

THE BEATLES
'I FEEL FINE'

WEEKS AT NUMBER ONE
5

FOLLOW-UP SINGLE: 'TICKET TO RIDE'
APRIL 1965

HIGHEST CHART POSITION
1

This was the third of three new Beatles singles in 1964, all of which went to number one. 'I Feel Fine' topped the Official Chart on 10 December when it replaced 'Little Red Rooster' by the Rolling Stones, who'd had a number-twelve hit the previous year with the Lennon–McCartney composition 'I Wanna Be Your Man'.

In April 1964, the Beatles occupied the entire top five on the US chart: 'Can't Buy Me Love', 'Twist and Shout', 'She Loves You', 'I Want to Hold Your Hand' and 'Please Please Me' ranked first to fifth, respectively. Once again, the Beatles also recorded a Christmas record for their fan club, with the 1964 edition including a performance of 'Jingle Bells'.

Scottish popsters Wet Wet Wet released a version of 'I Feel Fine' in 1990 as a double A-side single, coupled with 'Stay with Me Heartache'. It reached number thirty and failed to match the

---

1 January: *Top of the Pops* begins on BBC TV | 28 March: 'Pirate' station Radio Caroline begins

success of their recordings of 'With a Little Help from My Friends' (number one in May 1988) or 'Yesterday' (number four in August 1997). And perhaps proving that even the Beatles' B-sides are better than some A-sides, a version of 'She's a Woman', the 'I Feel Fine' flip, reached number twenty in April 1991 for Scritti Politti featuring Shabba Ranks.

NUMBER TWO
PETULA CLARK
'DOWNTOWN'

Born Sally Clark in Epsom, Surrey, Petula had her first top-forty hit in 1954 with 'The Little Shoemaker' and the first of two number ones in 1961 with 'Sailor'. 'Downtown' was written by Tony Hatch (composer of both the *Crossroads* and *Neighbours* theme tunes), who had intended to offer it to US soul group the Drifters (not to be confused with Cliff's backing band, who occupy the number-six slot in this year's top ten).

While Petula's recording was denied the Official Chart Christmas number one by the Beatles, she had her revenge in the US when 'Downtown' replaced 'I Feel Fine' at number one in January 1965. During her lengthy career, Petula covered several Beatles songs, including versions

1964
CHRISTMAS TOP TEN

1. **The Beatles**
'I Feel Fine'

2. **Petula Clark**
'Downtown'

3. **Val Doonican**
'Walk Tall'

4. **Gene Pitney**
'I'm Gonna Be Strong'

5. **Freddie and the Dreamers**
'I Understand'

6. **Cliff Richard and the Shadows**
'I Could Easily Fall'

7. **Georgie Fame and the Blue Flames**
'Yeh, Yeh'

8. **The Bachelors**
'No Arms Can Ever Hold You'

9. **P. J. Proby**
'Somewhere'

10. **Twinkle**
'Terry'

of 'The Fool on the Hill' and 'Rain', while 1969 saw her add backing vocals to the Plastic Ono Band's number-two single 'Give Peace a Chance', which was kept from the top by the Rolling Stones' 'Honky Tonk Woman'.

MANY HAPPY CHRISTMAS RETURNS

PART I

A dip into the Christmas selection box to find some of the songs we welcome back year after year, in one form or another...

Jimmy Boyd
'I Saw Mommy Kissing Santa Claus'
First top-forty peak: 3 (1953)
This gem from our 1953 Christmas top ten was written by Tommie Connor, who also wrote the Yuletide weepie 'The Little Boy that Santa Claus Forgot'. A version of that song sung by Vera Lynn featured in the 1982 film *Pink Floyd – The Wall*.

Johnny Mathis
'Winter Wonderland'
First top-forty peak: 17 (1958)
Johnny's was the only version of this seasonal favourite to break into the top forty, though many others have tried, including: Macy Gray; Earth, Wind & Fire; Billy Idol; Goldfrapp; Ringo Starr; and Snoop Dogg with Anna Kendrick.

Adam Faith
'Lonely Pup (In a Christmas Shop)'
First top-forty peak: 4 (1960)
This was the sixth of Adam's twenty-three top-forty singles, which also included the 1960 number five 'When Johnny Comes Marching Home', later appropriated by the Clash for their 1979 number twenty-five, 'English Civil War'.

Tommy Steele
'Must Be Santa'
First top-forty peak: 40 (1961)
Tommy's version scraped in at the bottom end of the top forty for one week, not helped by Joan Regan's rival recording the same year that reached number forty-two. Bob Dylan split the difference with his 2009 version, peaking at number forty-one.

Roy Orbison
'Pretty Paper'
First top-forty peak: 6 (1964)
Written by country music legend Willie Nelson, whose only top forty hit as a singer came with 'To All the Girls I've Loved Before', a 1984 number-seventeen duet with Julio Iglesias.

Max Bygraves
'Jingle Bell Rock'
First top-forty peak: 7 (1959)
The 1957 original by American singer Bobby Helm reached number six in the US, but took until 2020 to get to number twenty-seven in the UK. Sadly, no sight of Bobby's original B-side, 'Captain Santa Claus (and His Reindeer Space Patrol)'

Elvis Presley
'Blue Christmas'
First top-forty peak: 11 (1964)
Elvis's original has yet to break back into the top forty, despite five subsequent visits to the lower reaches of the Official Chart, though join us in Christmas 1982 for details of a Shakin' Stevens version that fared a little better...

Barron Knights
'Merry Gentle Pops'
First top-forty peak: 9 (1965)
This missed out on the 1964 Christmas top ten, but peaked at number nine in January 1965. It failed to return to the Official Chart, but the comedy quintet had another crack in 1980 with their number-seventeen single, 'Never Mind the Presents'.

John & Yoko and the Plastic Ono Band with the Harlem Community Choir
'Happy Xmas (War Is Over)'
First top-forty peak: 4 (1972)
This peaked at number two in 1980, following John's death, and was only kept from the top by a re-issue of John's 1975 single 'Imagine'. It has returned to the top forty on another seven occasions since then.

Wizzard
'I Wish It Could Be Christmas Everyday'
First top-forty peak: 4 (1973)
This has been a top-forty hit in fifteen different years. Additionally, a 2000 re-recording by the creative might of the Wombles' Mike Batt and Wizzard's Roy Wood ('I Wish It Could Be A Wombling Merry Christmas Every Day') reached number twenty-two.

Steeleye Span
'Gaudete'
First top-forty peak: 14 (1973)
So many categories to explore for this a cappella version of a sixteenth-century carol, sung entirely in Latin. One of two top-forty hits for British folk-rock group Steeleye Span, along with their 1975 number five, 'All Around My Hat'.

Elton John
'Step into Christmas'
First top-forty peak: 24 (1973)
A modest 1973 high of twenty-four gave this single little hint of future success, but the irresistible church- and sleigh-bell combination has returned it to the top forty five times, including a number-eight peak in both 2019 and 2020.

The Wombles
'Wombling Merry Christmas'
First top-forty peak: 2 (1975)
Kept from the top by Mud's 'Lonely This Christmas', this is one of the Wombles' nine hits (out of an overall total of eleven) to include the words 'Womble' or 'Wombling'.

Mike Oldfield
'In Dulci Jubilo'
First top-forty peak: 4 (1975)
An instrumental version of a twelfth-century German carol, this single reached its number-four peak in mid-January 1976, at which time Mike's best-selling *Tubular Bells* had barely begun its near four-year run on the Official Albums Chart.

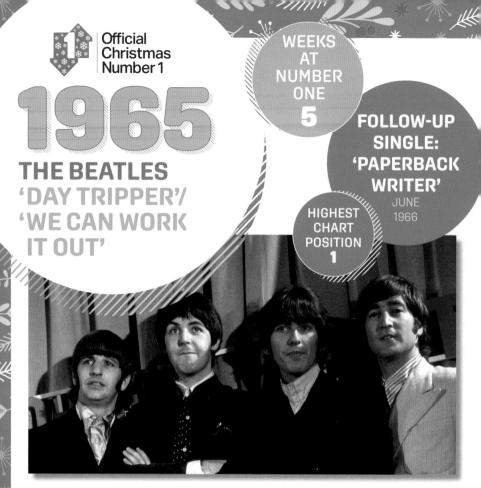

WEEKS AT NUMBER ONE
5

FOLLOW-UP SINGLE: 'PAPERBACK WRITER'
JUNE 1966

HIGHEST CHART POSITION
1

1965

THE BEATLES
'DAY TRIPPER'/
'WE CAN WORK IT OUT'

When the Beatles' ninth number one began its five-week stay at the top, the band became the first act to achieve three consecutive Christmas number ones – a feat that wouldn't be matched for another thirty-two years. 'Day Tripper'/'We Can Work It Out' was also the first double A-side single to be recognised by the Official Chart. It was released on 3 December, the same date as the Beatles' sixth studio album *Rubber Soul*, though neither

track featured. *Melody Maker* declared the dual-release event 'National Beatles Week'. Different chart rules in the US saw 'We Can Work It Out' become the band's eleventh number one, while 'Day Tripper' peaked at number five.

Cover versions of 'Day Tripper' include a 1966 recording by actress Mae West, who was immortalised the following year on the cover of the

24 January: Former prime minister Winston Churchill dies | 27 August: The Beatles have their only

Beatles' iconic *Sgt Pepper's Lonely Hearts Club Band* album.

A third Christmas record was issued to fan-club members in the UK on 17 December 1965. It was recorded in the small hours of Tuesday 9 November at the end of a session for George Harrison's song 'Think For Yourself' (working title: 'Won't Be There With You'). Alongside 'thank you' messages for cards and gifts received during the year, the record included an off-key a cappella rendition of 'Yesterday' (the Beatles' tenth US number one, though not released as a single in the UK until 1976 when it reached number eight), with John Lennon adopting a Scottish accent to sing 'Happy Christmas to Ya List'nas' and 'Auld Lang Syne'.

NUMBER TWO
CLIFF RICHARD
'WIND ME UP (LET ME GO)'

This ballad was Cliff's thirty-fifth top-forty single, the follow-up to 'The Time In Between', which was, at that time, his lowest-placed hit, having 'only' peaked at number twenty-two. 'Wind Me Up' spent three weeks at number two, constantly looking up at the Beatles. Cliff actually pre-dated the Fab Four when it came to re-recording singles for the German market: his 1960 number-two singles 'Fall in Love with You' and 'A Voice in

1965
CHRISTMAS TOP TEN

1 The Beatles
'Day Tripper'/'We Can Work It Out'

2 Cliff Richard
'Wind Me Up (Let Me Go)'

3 Ken Dodd
'The River'

4 The Seekers
'The Carnival Is Over'

5 Ken Dodd
'Tears'

6 Walker Brothers
'My Ship Is Coming In'

7 The Who
'My Generation'

8 Len Barry
'1-2-3'

9 The Toys
'A Lover's Concerto'

10 Four Seasons
'Let's Hang On'

the Wilderness' were released as 'Bin Verliebt' and 'Die Stimme der Liebe' in January 1961.

'Wind Me Up (Let Me Go)' was co-written by John C. Talley with Texan Bob Montgomery, a high school friend of Buddy Holly. Bob also co-wrote 'Heartbeat', which was a number-thirty single for Buddy in both 1959 and 1960, as well as a top-ten hit for Showaddywaddy in 1975 and Nick Berry in 1992.

1966

TOM JONES
'GREEN, GREEN GRASS OF HOME'

WEEKS AT NUMBER ONE
7

FOLLOW-UP SINGLE: 'DETROIT CITY'
FEBRUARY 1967

HIGHEST CHART POSITION
8

Following an Official Chart debut at number one with 'It's Not Unusual' in March 1965, 'Green, Green Grass of Home' became Tom's second chart-topper twenty months later, though it would be another forty-three years until his third. The song was written by Alabama-born Claude 'Curly' Putman – co-writer with Bobby Braddock of the country music classics 'D-I-V-O-R-C-E' and 'He Stopped Loving Her Today'.

'Green, Green Grass of Home' was first recorded by country singer Johnny Darrell, though Tom's version was inspired by his hero Jerry Lee Lewis, who recorded it for his 1965 album *Country Songs for City Folks*.

In early December, Tom's version knocked the Beach Boys' first number one, 'Good Vibrations', from the top spot. He remained

15 April: US magazine *Time* dubs London 'The Swinging City' | 30 July: England beat West Germany 4–2

at number one until mid-January 1967, replaced by the Monkees' 'I'm a Believer'. In the US, Tom peaked at number eleven (he would have his biggest hit there in 1971 with 'She's a Lady').

In 1967, Swedish group the Hootenanny Singers, featuring future ABBA member Björn Ulvaeus, recorded 'Green, Green Grass of Home' as 'En sång en gång för länge sen' ('A song once upon a time'), while a 1975 version by Elvis Presley reached number nine.

NUMBER TWO
DONOVAN
'SUNSHINE SUPERMAN'

While the UK release of Donovan's fourth top-forty hit was delayed by a contractual dispute, 'Sunshine Superman' went all the way to number one on the US *Billboard* Hot 100 chart in September 1966, replacing 'Summer in the City' by the Lovin' Spoonful. The recording featured future Led Zeppelin members Jimmy Page and John Paul Jones on electric guitar and bass guitar, respectively.

Donovan is credited with contributing the line 'sky of blue, sea of green' to 'Yellow Submarine' – a number one for the Beatles earlier in 1966 – and was also the inspiration for the song 'Donovan',

1966
CHRISTMAS TOP TEN

1. **Tom Jones**
'Green, Green Grass of Home'

2. **Donovan**
'Sunshine Superman'

3. **Dave Dee, Dozy, Beaky, Mick & Titch**
'Save Me'

4. **The Seekers**
'Morningtown Ride'

5. **The Kinks**
'Dead End Street'

6. **Val Doonican**
'What Would I Be'

7. **The Easybeats**
'Friday on My Mind'

8. **Jimmy Ruffin**
'What Becomes of the Brokenhearted'

9. **Elvis Presley**
'If Every Day Was Like Christmas'

10. **The Supremes**
'You Keep Me Hangin' On'

featured on the Happy Mondays' 1990 album, *Pills 'n' Thrills and Bellyaches*. Donovan himself made a return to the lower reaches of the Official Chart in 1990 when he collaborated with the Singing Corner (aka children's TV presenters Trevor and Simon) on a version of his hit 'Jennifer Juniper', which he originally took to number five in 1968.

to win the 1966 FIFA World Cup | 27 September: DJ Terry Wogan makes his debut on BBC radio

1967

THE BEATLES
'HELLO, GOODBYE'

FOLLOW-UP SINGLE:
MAGICAL MYSTERY TOUR (EP)
DECEMBER 1967

WEEKS AT NUMBER ONE
7

HIGHEST CHART POSITION
2

A fourth Christmas chart-topper for the Beatles, this was also their thirteenth number-one single and their longest spell at the top – seven weeks – since 1963's 'She Loves You'. Released on 24 November 1967, 'Hello, Goodbye' was the Beatles' first single following the death of their manager Brian Epstein the previous August. It entered the chart at number nine and rose to number one a week later, replacing 'Let the Heartaches Begin' by Long John Baldry, who had been a guest performer on the band's 1964 TV special, *Around the Beatles*. 'Hello, Goodbye' slipped to number eight at the end of January 1968 when 'The Ballad of Bonnie and Clyde' became Georgie Fame's third number-one single.

In addition to John, Paul, George and Ringo, 'Hello, Goodbye' featured viola players Leo Birnbaum and Kenneth Essex, both former

8 April: Sandie Shaw is the first UK winner of the Eurovision Song Contest with 'Puppet on a String' |

members of the London Symphony Orchestra. Kenneth was also a member of the string quartet that featured on the Beatles' 'Yesterday' and he played in the orchestra that backed ABBA's Eurovision Song Contest-winning performance of 'Waterloo' in 1974.

In 2014, the Cure recorded a version of 'Hello, Goodbye' with James McCartney, Paul's son, on piano.

NUMBER TWO
THE BEATLES
MAGICAL MYSTERY TOUR (EP)

Adding to the Fab Four's abundance of record-breaking statistics, the three weeks that this release spent at number two saw the Beatles emulate their Christmas 1963 Official Chart one–two success. In doing so, *Magical Mystery Tour* joined an extraordinary sequence of fifteen consecutive Beatles singles that peaked at number one or number two in the UK.

A six-song set, the EP also included the theme song to the band's third film, which premiered on BBC One on Boxing Day 1967. Unfortunately, the colourful adventure had its first airing in black and white, so its critical response didn't match the success of its music.

1967
CHRISTMAS TOP TEN

1. **The Beatles**
'Hello, Goodbye'

2. **The Beatles**
Magical Mystery Tour (EP)

3. **Tom Jones**
'I'm Coming Home'

4. **Val Doonican**
'If the Whole World Stopped Loving'

5. **Gene Pitney**
'Something's Gotten Hold of My Heart'

6. **Cliff Richard**
'All My Love'

7. **The Monkees**
'Daydream Believer'

8. **Long John Baldry**
'Let the Heartaches Begin'

9. **The Scaffold**
'Thank U Very Much'

10. **Four Tops**
'Walk Away Renée'

The film featured a performance by the Bonzo Dog Doo-Dah Band – see next year's Christmas top ten – plus a seat on the 'Mystery Tour' coach for Paul McCartney's brother, Mike McGear, who can be found in the 1967 Christmas top ten himself with his group the Scaffold…

30 September: 'Flowers in the Rain' by the Move is the first record played on the new BBC Radio 1

1968

THE SCAFFOLD
'LILY THE PINK'

FOLLOW-UP SINGLE: 'GIN GAN GOOLIE' JANUARY 1969

WEEKS AT NUMBER ONE 4

HIGHEST CHART POSITION 38

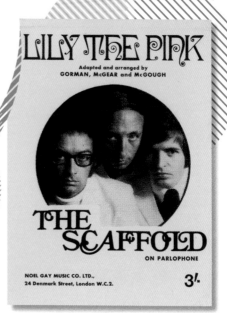

The third and biggest of five top-forty hits for Liverpool group the Scaffold, a music, poetry and comedy trio comprising poet, author and playwright Roger McGough, comedian John Gorman and the aforementioned Mike McGear. They first made an attempt at the Official Chart summit in 1967 when the Ariana Grande- and Prince-anticipating 'Thank U Very Much' peaked at number four. 'Lily the Pink' was a refined version of the drinking song 'The Ballad of Lydia Pinkham', a celebration of the American inventor of Pinkham's Vegetable Compound. The Scaffold adaptation, which featured Graham Nash of the Hollies on backing vocals, included the lyric 'Jennifer Eccles had terrible freckles' – a reference to the Hollies' 1968 single 'Jennifer Eccles'.

After three weeks at the top, 'Lily the Pink' dropped to number two on the first Official Chart of 1969 when it was replaced briefly by the Marmalade with 'Ob-La-Di, Ob-La-

18 April: London Bridge sold to American entrepreneur Robert P. McCulloch for £1,029,000 | 31 July: *Dad's*

Da' (co-written by Paul McCartney), before it returned for a fourth and final week.

'Gin Gan Goolie', the Scaffold's follow-up single, failed to emulate the success of its predecessor, though its B-side, 'Liver Birds', provided the theme to the eponymous long-running TV sitcom. John Gorman also returned to the Official Chart in 1980 when he reached number twenty-six with 'The Bucket of Water Song' by the Four Bucketeers – a spin-off from the ITV Saturday morning programme *Tiswas*. And 'Lily the Pink' had renewed interest, too, when, in 2006, former Liverpool FC and Republic of Ireland footballer John Aldridge won Irish talent show *Charity You're A Star* with his rendition of it. His cover even gave him a number-five hit in the Irish chart.

NUMBER TWO
THE FOUNDATIONS
'BUILD ME UP BUTTERCUP'

A 'coals to Newcastle' story for British soul band the Foundations, who just missed out on a second UK number one after 'Baby, Now That I Found You' spent two weeks at the top in November 1967, but managed a number-three hit in the US. They shared the top ten there with homegrown talent like Diana

1968
CHRISTMAS TOP TEN

1. The Scaffold
'Lily the Pink'

2. The Foundations
'Build Me Up Buttercup'

3. Nina Simone
'Ain't Got No, I Got Life'/'Do What You Gotta Do'

4. Des O'Connor
'1-2-3 O'Leary'

5. Love Sculpture
'Sabre Dance'

6. Bonzo Dog Doo-Dah Band
'I'm the Urban Spaceman'

7. Marmalade
'Ob-La-Di, Ob-La-Da'

8. Hugo Montenegro
'The Good, the Bad and the Ugly'

9. Fleetwood Mac
'Albatross'

10. Gun
'Race with the Devil'

Ross & the Supremes and Sly and the Family Stone.

'Build Me Up Buttercup' was the Foundations' first single to feature replacement singer Colin Young, following the departure of original singer Clem Curtis. The song was co-written by Tony Macaulay and Mike d'Abo – the latter a 'replacement', too, having taken over from Paul Jones to front Manfred Mann.

Army begins on **BBC One** | **26 September:** The film adaptation of Lionel Bart's musical *Oliver!* is released

Official Christmas Number 1

1969

ROLF HARRIS
'TWO LITTLE BOYS'

WEEKS AT NUMBER ONE
6

FOLLOW-UP SINGLE: 'STAIRWAY TO HEAVEN'
FEBRUARY 1993

HIGHEST CHART POSITION
7

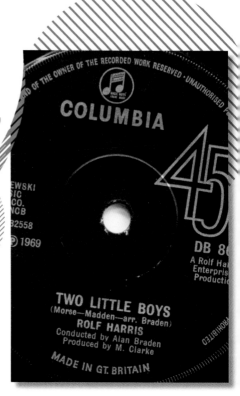

With lyrics by Edward Madden, whose credits include 'By the Light of the Silvery Moon' and the slightly less well-known 'I'd Rather Be a Lobster Than a Wise Guy', the last number one of the 'Swinging '60s' and the first of the '70s was a sentimental ballad written in 1902, telling the tale of heroic deeds in the American Civil War.

First popularised by Scottish vaudeville star Harry Lauder, the Rolf Harris version – his biggest hit since 'Sun Arise' peaked at number three in 1962 – was boosted by performances on his own TV show, which ran under various titles from 1967 until the early '80s.

When Prime Minister Margaret Thatcher appeared on BBC Radio Blackburn in 1979, she picked 'Two Little Boys' as her favourite song. Disappointingly, it was a year too early for her to have been talking

5 June: *The Italian Job*, starring Michael Caine and Noël Coward, is released | 3 July: Brian Jones of the

about the Splodgenessabounds version, which charted at number twenty-six in 1980 – the follow-up to their number-seven 'smash' 'Two Pints of Lager and a Packet of Crisps Please'.

'Two Little Boys' was a hit again in 2005 when a group of Hartlepool United fans, going under the name of Monkey Hangerz, took their version to number twenty-four. And Kenny Rogers recorded a version in 1971, too, when he was fronting the First Edition. Which brings us nicely to...

NUMBER TWO
KENNY ROGERS AND THE FIRST EDITION
'RUBY, DON'T TAKE YOUR LOVE TO TOWN'

Those not wishing to spend their Christmas record token on Rolf's tale of tragic gallantry could opt for the story of a wheelchair-bound Second World War veteran who looks on as his wife goes out for a night on the town.

Still eight years away from his first UK number one, with yet another heartbreaking tale, 'Lucille', Kenny Rogers fronted the First Edition, blending pop with country and folk music. This inevitably found a wider audience in the US, where the band had seven top-forty

1969
CHRISTMAS TOP TEN

1. **Rolf Harris**
'Two Little Boys'

2. **Kenny Rogers and the First Edition**
'Ruby, Don't Take Your Love to Town'

3. **The Archies**
'Sugar, Sugar'

4. **Elvis Presley**
'Suspicious Minds'

5. **Blue Mink**
'Melting Pot'

6. **Stevie Wonder**
'Yester-Me, Yester-You, Yesterday'

7. **Bobbie Gentry and Glen Campbell**
'All I Have to Do Is Dream'

8. **Engelbert Humperdinck**
'Winter World of Love'

9. **The Cufflinks**
'Tracy'

10. **Tom Jones**
'Without Love (There Is Nothing)'

hits, compared with just two in the UK. When the First Edition split, drummer Mickey Jones became an actor, with a bit part as 'Burly Miner' in the 1990 Arnold Schwarzenegger film *Total Recall*.

Rolling Stones dies | 5 October: *Monty Python's Flying Circus* begins on BBC One

SOME OLDE CURIOSITIES

PART I

A big Christmas hit can provide annual income and enjoyment for all involved, but, in a crowded market, it is easy to overlook some of the more left-field contributions…

The Goons
'I'm Walking Backwards for Christmas'
Chart peak: 4 (1956)
Fittingly, this was a hit in July. The Goons' follow-up single, 'The Ying Tong Song', went one better in the Official Chart, peaking at number three in October of the same year and returning to the top ten when it was re-issued in 1973.

Little Brenda Lee
'I'm Gonna Lasso Santa Claus'
Released: 1956 (did not chart)
While Brenda's 1962 number-six hit 'Rockin' Around the Christmas Tree' has returned to the top forty five times, this country variation on a festive theme has yet to reach as wide an audience. 'Little' Brenda's credit on the label of this, her first single, included the helpful description: '(9 years old)'.

Dick Emery
'A Cockney Christmas'
Released: 1960 (did not chart)
This rhyming-slang-laden knees-up around the 'old Joanna' features a musical arrangement by Ivor Raymonde, father of Simon from the Cocteau Twins, who make an appearance in Part II of this list.

Paddy Roberts
'Merry Christmas, You Suckers'
Released: 1962 (did not chart)
Unsurprisingly, this unashamedly cynical Yuletide message failed to add a third top-forty hit to Paddy's tally.

Christine Hunter
'Santa, Bring Me Ringo'
Released: 1964 (did not chart)
Another example of the extraordinary impact the Beatles had on pop culture in the first half of the '60s, this single is all the better for its B-side, 'Where Were You Daddy? (When Santa Got Stuck in the Chimney Chute)'.

The Go-Go's
'I'm Gonna Spend My Christmas with a Dalek'
Released: 1964 (did not chart)
The Go-Go's were a project for London producer and songwriter Johnny Worth, who eventually struck Official Chart gold when he wrote Jimmy Helms' 1973 number eight, 'Gonna Make You an Offer You Can't Refuse'.

Morecambe and Wise
'A-Wassailing'
Released: 1964 (did not chart)
For many years, *The Morecambe and Wise Show* was the most popular programme on the Christmas TV schedules, but neither this single nor the duo's 1967 recording of 'The Twelve Days of Christmas' troubled the Official Chart.

The Goodies
'Make a Daft Noise for Christmas'
Chart peak: 20 (1975)
This was the fifth of five top-forty hits in a twelve-month period for the TV comedy trio, who were at the height of their popularity. 'The Funky Gibbon', a UK number four, even crept into the lower end of the US *Billboard* Hot 100.

Chris Hill
'Bionic Santa'
Chart peak: 10 (1976)
The follow-up to 'Renta Santa', also a number ten the year before, this single was a hit for popular club DJ and record label executive Chris Hill, who made a third (unsuccessful) attempt on the Christmas chart in 1977 with 'Disco Santa'.

John Inman
'Rudolph the Red-Nosed Reindeer'
Released: 1976 (did not chart)
The TV sitcom star scraped into the top forty with his 1975 number thirty-nine, 'Are You Being Served, Sir?', but failed to chart with this festive offering.

The Dickies
'Silent Night'
Chart peak: 47 (1978)
This punk take on the traditional carol missed out on the top forty, but the Californian quintet went all the way to number seven with their next single, 'Banana Splits (Tra La La Song)'.

Clive Dunn
'Thinking of You This Christmas'
Released: 1978 (did not chart)
Despite a number of attempts, one-hit wonder Clive 'Corporal Jones' Dunn never managed to capitalise on the 1970 success of his chart-topping 'Grandad', which was taken from the album *Permission to Sing Sir*.

The Greedies
'A Merry Jingle'
Chart peak: 28 (1979)
This was the only record released by the curious alliance of Phil Lynott, Brian Downey and Scott Gorham of Thin Lizzy, in cahoots with Paul Cook and Steve Jones of the Sex Pistols.

WELCOME TO THE '70s

The charts for 1970 would suggest the market had split in two, with albums dominated by the more cultured talent of the Beatles, Led Zeppelin and Simon & Garfunkel, while singles' buyers were happy to take actor Lee Marvin's 'Wand'rin' Star' and the England World Cup squad's 'Back Home' to number one.

An estimated 600,000 people attended the 1970 Isle of Wight Festival, where Jimi Hendrix, the Doors and Joni Mitchell performed, while a more modest 1,500 rocked up to see T. Rex at the Pilton Pop, Blues & Folk Festival, mounted by Michael Eavis. In future years, the event would adopt the name of the nearby town of Glastonbury.

In 1972, a change in the law allowed the establishment of independent local radio, with new commercial stations launching in London and Glasgow before the end of 1973, followed by another fifteen across the UK over the next three years. The very first Radio 1 Roadshow also took place in 1973. Hosted by Alan 'Fluff' Freeman, it was beamed live from Cornwall to homes across the nation.

The middle of the decade saw 12-inch singles arrive in record shops – a format that had previously been the preserve of nightclub DJs, as it enabled them to stretch disco or reggae mixes out much further than a standard 7-inch single allowed. Later re-issues of the Donna Summer singles 'Love to Love You Baby' (sixteen minutes and fifty seconds) and 'I Feel Love' (fifteen minutes and forty-five seconds) were the apogee of this, though 1976 also saw a re-issue of the Who's 'Substitute' as a three-song 12-inch single. Within fifteen years, the format accounted for 32 per cent of all singles bought in the UK.

On the small screen, *Top of the Pops* continued to rule the roost, hitting a peak of 19 million viewers in 1979, helped in part by an industrial dispute that kept ITV off air for eleven weeks. Artists who had emerged in the previous decade were now considered safe enough to host their own TV shows, with Cilla Black, Cliff Richard and Lulu all given a platform to entertain the nation. The BBC also introduced *Seaside Special*, which ran for five years and offered airtime to Showaddywaddy, Peters and Lee, Lena Zavaroni, and the Wurzels. The show's theme tune, 'Summertime City', was written and sung by Womble-in-chief Mike Batt, providing him with his only solo hit in 1975.

Children's ITV offered the 'glam rock' era *Lift Off with Ayshea*, with a theme tune by Wizzard and a guest list that included David Bowie and Christmas number-one favourites Mud and Slade. The network followed this with a series of pop-star showcases, including the Bay City Rollers' 1975 show *Shang-a-Lang* and Marc Bolan's eponymous *Marc* in 1977. The T. Rex singer was past his Official Chart prime and the show did little to revive his fortunes, but it did give audiences a first chance to see the Jam, the Boomtown Rats and Generation X.

At the other end of the spectrum, rock and album tracks were championed by BBC TV's *The Old Grey Whistle Test* and later by the 'in concert' series *Rock Goes to College*. ITV countered with *So It Goes*, which gave the Sex Pistols their first ever TV appearance and featured performances by the Clash, the Buzzcocks, the Stranglers, and Siouxsie and the Banshees.

On the silver screen, the David Essex vehicles *That'll Be the Day* and *Stardust* contributed to a rock 'n' roll revival, T. Rex starred in the Ringo Starr-directed *Born to Boogie*, and the spring of 1975 brought premieres for *Slade in Flame* and the Who's *Tommy*. None of them had the impact of *Saturday Night Fever*, though, with its veritable 'greatest hits of disco' soundtrack that spent eighteen consecutive weeks atop the Official Albums Chart and provided the Bee Gees with four top-five singles, including their third number one, 'Night Fever'.

Just as the influence of *Saturday Night Fever* began to wane, along came *Grease*. The film's John Travolta and Olivia Newton-John duets 'You're the One That I Want' and 'Summer Nights' spent a combined total of sixteen weeks at number one, the second and third best-selling singles of 1978, beaten only by our Christmas number-one artist Boney M. with 'Rivers of Babylon'/'Brown Girl in the Ring'.

Seemingly immune to crazes and fads were ABBA, who had their first number one with the 1974 Eurovision Song Contest winner 'Waterloo' and then a further six chart-toppers before the decade was out. They even completed the Official Chart double – holding a number-one single and album simultaneously – on three occasions, with 'Fernando'/*Greatest Hits*, 'Knowing Me, Knowing You'/*Arrival* and 'Take a Chance on Me'/*The Album*.

And what of the noisy punks and their progeny? Conspiracy theorists had a field day in June 1977 when, at the height of the Queen's Silver Jubilee celebrations, the Sex Pistols' 'God Save the Queen' was kept from the number-one spot by Rod Stewart's double A-side 'I Don't Want to Talk About It'/'The First Cut Is the Deepest'. (Rumours of chart manipulation proved unfounded, although Rod was given a knighthood in 2016…) The Boomtown Rats, Blondie, Ian Dury and the Blockheads, and the Police would all have spells at number one, too, with sales boosted by a new trend for coloured vinyl singles, while the Cars' 1978 number three, 'My Best Friend's Girl', was helped by a reintroduction of the picture disc format.

All this excitement saw 1978 become the biggest year ever for sales of singles. However, numbers grew even more the following year when into this heady brew came the Sugarhill Gang – scoring the UK's first ever top-ten rap hit with 'Rapper's Delight' – plus debuts for the Specials, the Selecter and Madness.

In October 1979, the Buggles sat at number one, proclaiming that 'Video Killed the Radio Star'. That same year, Sony launched the Walkman cassette player, songs and hair got shorter, and there was a school of thought that 'new wave' was where it was at. Surely the charts would belong to the kids from now on and every Christmas number one would be a million-selling electro, two-tone or rap classic?

Let's find out…

Official Christmas Number 1

1970

DAVE EDMUNDS
'I HEAR YOU KNOCKING'

FOLLOW-UP SINGLE: 'BABY I LOVE YOU'
JANUARY 1973

WEEKS AT NUMBER ONE
6

HIGHEST CHART POSITION
8

Dave Edmunds, as part of one-hit wonder Love Sculpture, had his first taste of Official Chart success in the Christmas top ten of 1968 with a rocking number-five version of Khachaturian's ballet melody 'Sabre Dance'. 'I Hear You Knocking' was originally recorded in 1955 by New Orleans rhythm and blues singer Smiley Lewis, who gets a namecheck on Dave's version, as do Fats Domino, Chuck Berry and Huey 'Piano' Smith.

The single rose to number one at the end of November 1970 when it displaced Jimi Hendrix's posthumous chart-topper 'Voodoo Chile'. It hung on for six weeks until the record-buying public decided that Clive Dunn's 'Grandad' was more to their taste.

26 January: Simon & Garfunkel release their *Bridge over Troubled Water* album | 19 September:

Dave was the sixth Welsh artist to top the Official Chart. The fifth was Amen Corner –'(If Paradise Is) Half as Nice', 1969 – whose singer Andy Fairweather Low made a guest appearance on Dave's 1971 solo album, *Rockpile*.

The seventh was future Christmas-number-one club member Shakin' Stevens, who wouldn't claim the honour until the 1980s, though 1970 did see he and the Sunsets release *A Legend*, their debut album, which was produced by Dave and even included a version of 'I Hear You Knocking'. Dave's other production credits include Stray Cats, whose chart debut, 'Runaway Boys', was a Christmas 1980 top-ten hit.

NUMBER TWO
McGUINNESS FLINT
'WHEN I'M DEAD AND GONE'

This was the first of two top-ten hits for McGuinness Flint – the other, 'Malt and Barley Blues', reached number five in 1971.

The band's slightly misleading name suggests they were simply a duo – Tom McGuinness, former Manfred Mann guitarist, and Hughie Flint, drummer with John Mayall & the Bluesbreakers during Eric Clapton's tenure – yet the line-up was actually a quintet, also

1970
CHRISTMAS TOP TEN

1. **Dave Edmunds**
   'I Hear You Knocking'

2. **McGuinness Flint**
   'When I'm Dead and Gone'

3. **Neil Diamond**
   'Cracklin' Rosie'

4. **Glen Campbell**
   'It's Only Make Believe'

5. **Jackson 5**
   'I'll Be There'

6. **Clive Dunn**
   'Grandad'

7. **Andy Williams**
   'Home Lovin' Man'

8. **Gilbert O'Sullivan**
   'Nothing Rhymed'

9. **Gerry Monroe**
   'My Prayer'

10. **Chairmen of the Board**
    '(You've Got Me) Dangling on a String'

including Dennis Coulson, Benny Gallagher and Graham Lyle. Hit-making pair Gallagher and Lyle would go on to have two number-six successes of their own in 1976 with 'I Wanna Stay with You' and 'Heart on My Sleeve'. Graham later wrote several of Tina Turner's biggest hits, including the 1989 Christmas number eight, 'I Don't Wanna Lose You'.

The first Glastonbury Festival is held | 23 November: Presenter and DJ Zoe Ball born

Official Christmas Number 1

1971

BENNY HILL
'ERNIE (THE FASTEST MILKMAN IN THE WEST)'

FOLLOW-UP SINGLE: 'ERNIE (THE FASTEST MILKMAN IN THE WEST)'
MAY 1992

WEEKS AT NUMBER ONE
4

HIGHEST CHART POSITION
29

The Official Chart of Christmas 1971 was topped by a tale of love and loss, with milkman Ernie and baker Two-Ton Ted fighting for the affections of widow Sue, only for tragedy to strike in the shape of a stale pork pie. This was Benny's fourth top-forty hit, following his Official Chart debut ten years previously with the number-twelve single 'Gather in the Mushrooms'.

The label for 'Ernie' includes a credit for vocal trio the Ladybirds, who were the 'in-house' backing singers at *Top of the Pops* between 1966 and 1978 and featured on Sandie Shaw's Eurovision-winning 1967 number one, 'Puppet on a String'.

In the accompanying video for 'Ernie', the role of Two-Ton Ted was played by Henry McGee, Benny's

20 January: Singer and songwriter Gary Barlow born | 10 March: *Get Carter*, crime drama starring Michael

regular 'straight man' partner, with both men appearing in the 1969 film *The Italian Job*. Benny was born in Southampton in 1924 – the son and grandson of circus clowns – and his pre-fame employment included working in the local Woolworths store and delivering milk in a horse-drawn cart for a nearby dairy.

In 1987, Genesis made a video for 'Anything She Does', a track from their *Invisible Touch* album, with Benny as Fred Scuttle, the band's head of security. Michael Jackson was also a big fan, taking time out from a UK trip in 1992 (the same year he reached Christmas number one) to visit Benny in hospital.

NUMBER TWO
T. REX
'JEEPSTER'

This was the second single from T. Rex's chart-topping album *Electric Warrior*, which also contained 'Get It On', the second of the band's three number-one singles. 'Jeepster' spent five non-consecutive weeks at number two – one week behind Slade's 'Coz I Luv You', then four more behind 'Ernie'.

Electric Warrior includes a credit for 23-year-old tape operator Martin Rushent, who returns to our story in ten years' time as producer of

1971
CHRISTMAS TOP TEN

 Benny Hill
'Ernie (The Fastest Milkman in the West)'

 T. Rex
'Jeepster'

 Slade
'Coz I Luv You'

 Isaac Hayes
'Theme from *Shaft*'

 Gilbert O'Sullivan
'No Matter How I Try'

 John Kongos
'Tokoloshe Man'

 Cilla Black
'Something Tells Me (Something's Gonna Happen Tonight)'

 Cher
'Gypsys, Tramps & Thieves'

 Olivia Newton-John
'Banks of the Ohio'

 Tom Jones
'Till'

the 1981 Christmas number one. And, as for the aforementioned Ladybirds, the vocal trio were among a variety of session musicians who provided backing on 'The Wizard' – the 1965 debut single of Marc Bolan, the frontman of T. Rex.

Official Christmas Number 1

1972

LITTLE JIMMY OSMOND
'LONG HAIRED LOVER FROM LIVERPOOL'

FOLLOW-UP SINGLE: 'TWEEDLE DEE'
MARCH 1973

WEEKS AT NUMBER ONE 5

HIGHEST CHART POSITION 4

James Arthur Osmond was just nine years and eight months of age when his debut single hit the Official Chart summit on 17 December 1972. To date, he is the youngest artist ever to have a number-one single, while the youngest female artist to top the Official Chart is Helen Shapiro with 'Walkin' Back to Happiness' (a song that featured in our Christmas 1961 top ten).

Not content with their youngest sibling holding the top spot, the Osmonds – brothers Alan, Donny, Jay, Merrill and Wayne – were at number five with 'Crazy Horses', while Donny was also at number nine with 'Why', the third of thirteen solo top-forty hits. (And you are only a turn of the page away from sister Marie's 1973 chart debut, 'Paper Roses'…)

9 August: Tim Rice and Andrew Lloyd Webber's musical *Jesus Christ Superstar* has its London premiere |

Jimmy belongs to a select club of just three pairs of siblings who have both achieved solo number ones separately. He, of course, features alongside Donny, who topped the chart in 1972 with 'Puppy Love' and again in 1973 with 'The Twelfth of Never' and 'Young Love'. The Bedingfields were next, with Daniel's 'Gotta Get Thru This' claiming the top spot in 2001 (followed by 'If You're Not the One' in 2002 and 'Never Gonna Leave Your Side' in 2003), while sister Natasha went straight in at number one in August 2004 with 'These Words'. And the very first sibling pairing was Eden Kane (aka Richard Sarstedt) and his younger brother Peter Sarstedt with, respectively, 'Well I Ask You' (1961) and 'Where Do You Go To (My Lovely)?' (1969).

NUMBER TWO
CHUCK BERRY
'MY DING-A-LING'

Chuck's only number one – fifteen years after he made his Official Chart debut with 'School Day (Ring! Ring! Goes the Bell)' – spent four weeks at the top before falling behind Little Jimmy. The song was also Chuck's only number one in the US, where he had first charted in 1955 with 'Maybellene'.

'My Ding-a-Ling' was written by Dave Bartholomew – the man

1972
CHRISTMAS TOP TEN

1. **Little Jimmy Osmond**
'Long Haired Lover from Liverpool'

2. **Chuck Berry**
'My Ding-a-Ling'

3. **T. Rex**
'Solid Gold Easy Action'

4. **John & Yoko and the Plastic Ono Band with the Harlem Community Choir**
'Happy Xmas (War Is Over)'

5. **The Osmonds**
'Crazy Horses'

6. **Slade**
'Gudbuy T'Jane'

7. **Elton John**
'Crocodile Rock'

8. **Michael Jackson**
'Ben'

9. **Donny Osmond**
'Why'

10. **Moody Blues**
'Nights in White Satin'

responsible for our 1970 Christmas number one 'I Hear You Knocking' – and the single was recorded live at the Lanchester Arts Festival, where Chuck topped a bill that also included Slade and Pink Floyd.

Chuck's 1963 seasonal offering, 'Run Rudolph Run', peaked at number thirty-six and reappeared in the lower reaches of the Official Chart in 2019.

11 September: Magnus Magnusson presents the first episode of BBC quiz show *Mastermind*

1973

SLADE
'MERRY XMAƧ EVERYBODY'

FOLLOW-UP SINGLE: 'EVERYDAY'
APRIL 1974

WEEKS AT NUMBER ONE
5

HIGHEST CHART POSITION
3

This song began life in 1967 as Noddy Holder's unused tale of a rocking chair. But, in December 1973, 'Merry Xmaƨ Everybody' – the lyrics re-written one night at Noddy's parents' house and the track recorded on a humid September day in New York – became Slade's biggest and final number one.

'Merry Xmaƨ Everybody' has now spent a total of more than two years in the Official Chart. While the age of streaming has neglected to return it to the top ten (a number-sixteen peak in 2017 is the closest so far), the song did manage a sort-of return to number one in December 1989 when Jive Bunny and the Mastermixers sampled it in their third chart-topper of that year, 'Let's Party'.

From their first number one, 'Coz I Luv You' in November 1971, until 'Far Far Away' in November 1974, Slade's run of consecutive hits included six number ones, three

1 March: Pink Floyd release their eighth album, *The Dark Side of the Moon* | 4 June: Noel Edmonds

number twos, two number threes and one 'lowly' number four ('Look Wot You Dun').

With seven of those singles featuring the band's 'graffiti on bog walls' trademark (mis)spelling, editors and spell-checkers also had to contend with the backwards 's' of 'Merry Xmaꙅ Everybody', plus the reversed 'n' of its B-side, 'Don't Blame Me', just for good measure.

Earlier in 1973, when 'Cum on Feel the Noize' and 'Skweeze Me, Pleeze Me' both debuted at the top, Slade became the first act to enter the Official Chart at number one with consecutive releases.

NUMBER TWO
GARY GLITTER
'I LOVE YOU LOVE ME LOVE'

The second of Gary Glitter's three number ones, 'I Love You Love Me Love' spent four weeks at the top before Slade swept the competition aside on 9 December. It was co-written by in-demand producer Mike Leander, whose string arrangement on the *Sgt Pepper* track 'She's Leaving Home' saw harpist Sheila Bromberg become the first female musician to play on a Beatles recording.

In 1987, Mike also co-wrote Tom Jones's number-two hit 'A

1973
CHRISTMAS TOP TEN

1 Slade
'Merry Xmaꙅ Everybody'

2 Gary Glitter
'I Love You Love Me Love'

3 New Seekers feat. Lyn Paul
'You Won't Find Another Fool Like Me'

4 Wizzard
'I Wish It Could Be Christmas Everyday'

5 Alvin Stardust
'My Coo Ca Choo'

6 Marie Osmond
'Paper Roses'

7 Leo Sayer
'The Show Must Go On'

8 David Essex
'Lamplight'

9 Mott the Hoople
'Roll Away the Stone'

10 Roxy Music
'Street Life'

Boy from Nowhere' with Edward Seago, the man responsible for the English lyrics to Eurodisco 'favourite' 'Y Viva España'.

A special mention must also go to Wizzard's festive favourite, 'I Wish It Could Be Christmas Everyday', which peaked at number four this year and spent four consecutive weeks in fourth place.

succeeds Tony Blackburn as presenter of *Radio 1 Breakfast*

1974

MUD
'LONELY THIS CHRISTMAS'

FOLLOW-UP SINGLE: 'THE SECRETS THAT YOU KEEP' FEBRUARY 1975

WEEKS AT NUMBER ONE 4

HIGHEST CHART POSITION 3

The second of Mud's three number ones, 'Lonely This Christmas' replaced Barry White at the summit in mid-December and stayed there for the next month. Readers of a certain age may recall the band's *Top of the Pops* appearance, which featured a pair of Christmas bauble earrings on guitarist Rob Davis, stagehands on step ladders sprinkling fake snow, and a ventriloquist dummy on the knee of singer Les Gray

delivering the spoken middle eight of the song.

Following Slade in 1973, this marks one of only two occasions on which we had 'Christmas'- or 'Xmas'-titled songs at number one in consecutive years. You will have to wait until 1984–85 for the second instance.

Prepare to be impressed as you learn that 'Lonely This Christmas'

5 January: Saturday morning children's programme *Tiswas* begins on ITV | 13 February: Singer and

songwriters Nicky Chinn and Mike Chapman are also responsible for Mud's previous number one, 'Tiger Feet', as well as the song that knocked it off the top spot, Suzi Quatro's 'Devil Gate Drive', in addition to hits by Sweet ('Block Buster!'), Toni Basil ('Mickey'), Exile ('Kiss You All Over') and Smokie ('Living Next Door to Alice').

Mud guitarist Rob Davis had to wait until 2000 for his first number-one songwriting credit, but he can now boast Fragma's 'Toca's Miracle', Spiller's 'Groovejet (If This Ain't Love)' and Kylie Minogue's 'Can't Get You Out of My Head'.

NUMBER TWO
BACHMAN–TURNER OVERDRIVE
'YOU AIN'T SEEN NOTHING YET'

This was one of two top-forty hits for Canadian rockers Bachman–Turner Overdrive. Beginning life as Brave Belt, the band went on to adopt the surnames of members the Bachman brothers (Randy and Robbie) and Fred (C.F.) Turner.

'You Ain't Seen Nothing Yet' had a two-week run at number two before it slipped quietly from the Official Chart to become a staple of 'dad rock' and driving-themed

1974
CHRISTMAS TOP TEN

1 **Mud**
'Lonely This Christmas'

2 **Bachman–Turner Overdrive**
'You Ain't Seen Nothing Yet'

3 **The Rubettes**
'Juke Box Jive'

4 **Barry White**
'You're the First, the Last, My Everything'

5 **The Wombles**
'Wombling Merry Christmas'

6 **Ralph McTell**
'Streets of London'

7 **Elvis Presley**
'My Boy'

8 **Disco Tex and the Sex-O-Lettes**
'Get Dancin''

9 **Gary Glitter**
'Oh Yes! You're Beautiful'

10 **Hello**
'Tell Him'

compilations. It had a revival in the mid-'90s when parody DJs Mike Smash and Dave Nice repeatedly faded it in with a push of their giant lever and it then reappeared ten years later as the theme tune for TV coverage of Formula 1 motor racing.

Meanwhile, at number seven, 'My Boy' – Elvis Presley's eighty-ninth top-forty hit – marked the final Christmas top-ten appearance for 'The King'.

THE CHRISTMAS HITS IN NUMBERS

PART I

1

Instrumental Christmas number one (Winifred Atwell, 'Let's Have Another Party')

Christmas number one in the UK and US simultaneously (Whitney Houston, 'I Will Always Love You')

Christmas top-ten song title containing the word 'snow' (Russ Conway, 'Snow Coach')

2

Christmas number ones by fictional or non-human characters (Mr Blobby; Bob the Builder)

Christmas number-one duets (Renée and Renato; Robbie Williams and Nicole Kidman)

5

Christmas number ones with 'love' in the title ('I Love You'; 'Long Haired Lover from Liverpool'; 'Save Your Love'; 'I Will Always Love You'; 'I Love Sausage Rolls')

Christmas one-hit wonders (number-one artists who have yet to return to the top 100)

Christmas one-hit wonders who donated their proceeds to charity

7

Christmas number ones featuring Paul McCartney

Christmas number ones with 'Christmas' (or 'Xmas') in the title

Christmas number ones by *X Factor* winners

Characters in the shortest Christmas number-one song titles ('Only You'; 'Too Much'; 'Goodbye'; 'Perfect')

3

Songs that have been Christmas number one more than once ('Do They Know It's Christmas'; 'Mary's Boy Child'; 'Bohemian Rhapsody')

Consecutive Christmas number ones for the Beatles, the Spice Girls and LadBaby

Christmas number ones by Welsh artists (Tom Jones; Dave Edmunds; Shakin' Stevens)

4

Christmas number twos for Cliff Richard ('The Next Time'/'Bachelor Boy'; 'Wind Me Up (Let Me Go)'; 'Daddy's Home'; 'The Millennium Prayer')

8

Unique Christmas top-ten hits for Madonna

Weeks that Wham!'s 'Last Christmas' spent at number two before finally reaching number one in 2021

9

Years of age of Little Jimmy Osmond when he claimed the 1972 Christmas number one

Consecutive weeks at number one for Whitney Houston's 'I Will Always Love You'

10

Christmas number ones that were also the year's best-selling single

All figures correct as of May 2021.

1975

QUEEN 'BOHEMIAN RHAPSODY'

FOLLOW-UP SINGLE: 'YOU'RE MY BEST FRIEND'
JULY 1976

WEEKS AT NUMBER ONE 9

HIGHEST CHART POSITION 7

Queen's bass player, had bailed before the final collaboration with Abz and co.

Queen's first number one was their fourth top-forty single and the first of a total of six number ones, though three were aided by the appearance of other artists: David Bowie on 'Under Pressure' in 1981; George Michael and Lisa Stansfield on *Five Live* (EP) in 1993; and Five on 'We Will Rock You' in 2000. The last two were made without frontman (and 'Bohemian Rhapsody' songwriter) Freddie Mercury, while John Deacon,

'Bohemian Rhapsody' was a little less successful in the US, peaking at number nine in April 1976, though it hit a new chart peak of number two in September 1992, helped by its use in the film *Wayne's World*.

While the inclusion of a large gong arguably atones for the lack of sleigh bells, 'Bohemian Rhapsody' is definitely an unusual Christmas hit in many respects, not least because its runtime of almost six minutes makes it the

4 April: Sitcom *The Good Life* begins on BBC One | 20 June: Steven Spielberg's film *Jaws* opens in

longest of all our Christmas number ones. (It is, however, still three minutes and forty-three seconds shorter than the longest number one of all time, 'All Around the World' by Oasis, which topped the Official Chart in January 1998.) Additionally, it has no chorus and doesn't even mention the song title in its lyrics, though it does mention the title of the song that replaced it at number one – ABBA's 'Mamma Mia'.

'Bohemian Rhapsody' returned to the top ten in 2005, courtesy of vocal quartet G4, but the 2009 Muppets version could only manage number thirty-two. Queen's original version enjoyed a new lease of life following the release of the 2018 film *Bohemian Rhapsody*, peaking at number forty-five that November.

NUMBER TWO
GREG LAKE
'I BELIEVE IN FATHER CHRISTMAS'

A one-hit wonder as a solo artist, Greg had to settle for number two again as part of Emerson, Lake & Palmer when the prog-rock band's 'Fanfare for the Common Man' was kept from the top in July 1977 by Hot Chocolate's 'So You Win Again'. Greg and Hot Chocolate (this time with 'You Sexy Thing') were two of four acts to hold the number-two spot during the nine-week reign of 'Bohemian Rhapsody'. The other

1975
CHRISTMAS TOP TEN

1. **Queen**
'Bohemian Rhapsody'

2. **Greg Lake**
'I Believe in Father Christmas'

3. **Laurel and Hardy with the Avalon Boys feat. Chill Wills**
'The Trail of the Lonesome Pine'

4. **Dana**
'It's Gonna be a Cold Cold Christmas'

5. **Chubby Checker**
'Let's Twist Again'/'The Twist'

6. **Demis Roussos**
'Happy to Be on an Island in the Sun'

7. **Hot Chocolate**
'You Sexy Thing'

8. **The Stylistics**
'Na Na Is the Saddest Word'

9. **David Bowie**
'Golden Years'

10. **Chris Hill**
'Renta Santa'

two were Laurel and Hardy ('The Trail of the Lonesome Pine') and Sailor ('A Glass of Champagne').

The lyrics to 'I Believe in Father Christmas' were written by Pete Sinfield, who would later apply his talent to number-one singles by Bucks Fizz ('The Land of Make Believe', 1981) and Celine Dion ('Think Twice', 1994).

1976

JOHNNY MATHIS
'WHEN A CHILD IS BORN (SOLEADO)'

FOLLOW-UP SINGLE: 'TOO MUCH, TOO LITTLE, TOO LATE'
MARCH 1978

WEEKS AT NUMBER ONE
3

HIGHEST CHART POSITION
3

Johnny Mathis's only number one began life as 'Soleado', a 1974 single by Italian group the Daniel Sentacruz Ensemble, before Austrian Fred Jay – lyric writer for Boney M.'s 'Ma Baker' and 'Rasputin' – gave it a Christmas makeover. Having dethroned Showaddywaddy, Johnny spent three weeks at the top until he was replaced by David Soul with 'Don't Give Up on Us'.

'When a Child Is Born (Soleado)' failed to chart in the US, yet Johnny's biggest hit there –'Chances Are', a 1957 number one – suffered the same fate in the UK. In 1981, Johnny re-recorded 'When a Child Is Born' as a duet with Gladys Knight.

Johnny made his Official Chart debut with the single 'Teacher, Teacher', which reached number

23 February: English artist L. S. Lowry dies, aged eighty-eight | 2 October: Saturday morning children's

twenty-seven in 1958 – the same year he had his first Christmas hit. (His rendition of seasonal favourite 'Winter Wonderland' is still the only version of the song to have charted in the UK top forty.) It was also the year he released his album *Johnny's Greatest Hits* in the US, where it notched up 490 non-consecutive weeks on the Billboard album chart – a record that was only surpassed in 1983 by Pink Floyd's *The Dark Side of the Moon*.

Since then, Johnny has added to his album catalogue with the festive offerings *Give Me Your Love for Christmas*, *Christmas Eve with Johnny Mathis*, *The Christmas Album* and *Sending You a Little Christmas*.

NUMBER TWO
SHOWADDYWADDY
'UNDER THE MOON OF LOVE'

This was the sole number one – but one of twenty-three top-forty hits between 1974 and 1982 – for Leicester rock 'n' roll revivalists Showaddywaddy. The band formed in 1973 following the amalgamation of two groups, Choise and Golden Hammer, which resulted in the line-up consisting of two singers, two guitarists, two bass players and two drummers.

Their more obvious festive release, 'Hey Mister Christmas', peaked

1976
CHRISTMAS TOP TEN

1. **Johnny Mathis**
'When a Child Is Born (Soleado)'

2. **Showaddywaddy**
'Under the Moon of Love'

3. **ABBA**
'Money, Money, Money'

4. **Queen**
'Somebody to Love'

5. **Mike Oldfield**
'Portsmouth'

6. **Electric Light Orchestra**
'Livin' Thing'

7. **Yvonne Elliman**
'Love Me'

8. **Tina Charles**
'Dr Love'

9. **Smokie**
'Living Next Door to Alice'

10. **Chris Hill**
'Bionic Santa'

at number thirteen in 1974, but 'Under the Moon of Love' had topped the Official Chart for three weeks earlier in December, denying Queen their second number one with 'Somebody to Love'. The song was originally a minor US hit in 1961 for Curtis Lee and was co-written with Tommy Boyce, whose own credits include the Monkees' 'Last Train to Clarksville'.

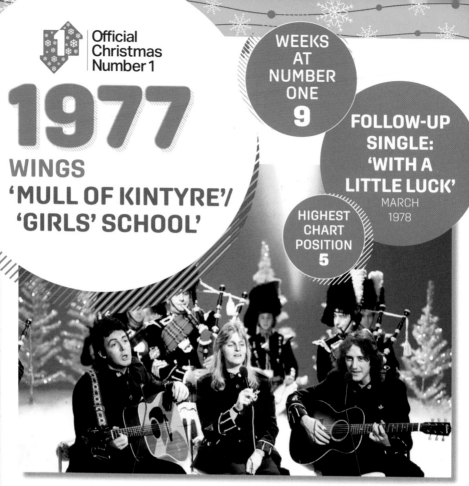

Official Christmas Number 1

1977

WINGS
'MULL OF KINTYRE'/ 'GIRLS' SCHOOL'

WEEKS AT NUMBER ONE
9

FOLLOW-UP SINGLE: 'WITH A LITTLE LUCK'
MARCH 1978

HIGHEST CHART POSITION
5

Recorded during the sessions for 1978's *London Town* album, 'Mull of Kintyre' was inspired by the Scottish Kintyre peninsula on which Paul McCartney has owned a remote rural retreat since the mid-'60s. The song itself was recorded in a makeshift mobile studio in the farm's barn, with the nearby Campbeltown Pipe Band providing local colour and distinctive musical accompaniment.

Originally unconvinced as to its hit potential, the single was coupled with the rockier – and more lyrically questionable – 'Girls' School' as a double A-sided release.

Maintaining the number-one position for nine weeks between 1977 and 1978, 'Mull of Kintyre' sold over 2 million copies in the UK and – until being surpassed by Band Aid in 1984 – was the

15 February: Children's art programme *Take Hart*, with Tony Hart and Aardman Animations character

biggest-selling single of all time. Paul features elsewhere on the all-time physical best-sellers list, too, with the Beatles appearing at number nine ('She Loves You') and number eighteen ('I Want to Hold Your Hand'), while his erstwhile partner in all things Fab, John Lennon, resides at number twenty with the 1971 single 'Imagine'.

NUMBER TWO
BRIGHOUSE AND RASTRICK
BRASS BAND
'THE FLORAL DANCE'

Formed around 1881 in the West Riding of Yorkshire, the Brighouse and Rastrick Brass Band may qualify as the longest-running group to ever grace the Official Chart, even if any original members are now long gone. Their instrumental version of 'The Floral Dance' was a Christmas hit in 1977, spending six weeks at number two behind Wings and selling over half a million copies. The following Christmas, thinking he could hear the curious tone of the cornet, clarinet and big trombone, DJ and TV presenter Terry Wogan reached number twenty-one with his own unique vocal take on the brass-driven standard.

Originally written in 1911 by musician and composer Katie Moss, 'The Floral Dance' tells the story of Katie's experience at the annual 'Furry Dance', which takes place to this day in the town of Helston, Cornwall.

Also gracing the top ten was the first Official Chart entry for Bing Crosby's 'White Christmas' – a mere thirty-five years after he first recorded it.

1977
CHRISTMAS TOP TEN

1. **Wings**
'Mull of Kintyre'/'Girls' School'

2. **Brighouse and Rastrick Brass Band**
'The Floral Dance'

3. **Bee Gees**
'How Deep Is Your Love'

4. **Ruby Winters**
'I Will'

5. **Bing Crosby**
'White Christmas'

6. **Donna Summer**
'Love's Unkind'

7. **Bonnie Tyler**
'It's a Heartache'

8. **Darts**
'Daddy Cool'

9. **Jonathan Richman and the Modern Lovers**
'Egyptian Reggae'

10. **Hot Chocolate**
'Put Your Love In Me'

Morph, begins on BBC One | 16 September: Singer Marc Bolan of T. Rex dies, aged twenty-nine

Official Christmas Number 1

1978

BONEY M.
'MARY'S BOY CHILD/ OH MY LORD'

FOLLOW-UP SINGLE: 'PAINTER MAN'
MARCH 1979

WEEKS AT NUMBER ONE
4

HIGHEST CHART POSITION
10

Undoubtedly, 1978 was an extremely successful year for Boney M., with two Official Chart number-one hits – the double A-side 'Rivers of Babylon'/'Brown Girl in the Ring' and the medley 'Mary's Boy Child/Oh My Lord' – both selling a million copies. The former also became the year's best-selling single, despite serious competition from John Travolta and Olivia Newton-John. (The duo's 'Summer Nights' did keep Boney M.'s

'Rasputin' at number two, though.) 'Mary's Boy Child/Oh My Lord' re-charted in 2007, but *Daddy Cool*, the Boney M. 'jukebox' musical that opened in London the previous year, closed after just six months.

Boney M. were conceived by German composer and producer Frank Farian when the European success of his single 'Do You Wanna Bump' persuaded him to assemble

8 March: *The Hitchhiker's Guide to the Galaxy* begins on BBC Radio 4 | 14 December: *Superman,*

a group to front his project. Four Caribbean singers – Marcia Barrett and Liz Mitchell from Jamaica, Maizie Williams from Montserrat and the flamboyant Bobby Farrell from Aruba – were recruited, though only Marcia and Liz sang on future recordings, with Frank providing male vocals. However, Frank's 1990 attempt to repeat this winning formula with Milli Vanilli ended in controversy when he was forced to admit that dancers Rob Pilatus and Fab Morvan were miming to his recordings, resulting in the revocation of their Grammy Award for Best New Artist.

NUMBER TWO
VILLAGE PEOPLE
'Y.M.C.A.'

After three weeks biding their time, Village People landed their only number-one hit in the last Official Chart of 1978, beginning a three-week run at the top. They were denied a second number one in 1979 when 'In the Navy' was kept at number two by Gloria Gaynor's 'I Will Survive'.

Like Boney M., Village People began as a vehicle for producer Jacques Morali, with singer/lyricist/motorcycle cop Victor Willis the only original performer. By the time they recorded 'Y.M.C.A.', though, Village People's line-up featured backing vocals from cowboy Randy Jones,

1978
CHRISTMAS TOP TEN

1. **Boney M.**
'Mary's Boy Child/Oh My Lord'

2. **Village People**
'Y.M.C.A.'

3. **Barron Knights**
'A Taste of Aggro'

4. **Bee Gees**
'Too Much Heaven'

5. **Barbra Streisand and Neil Diamond**
'You Don't Bring Me Flowers'

6. **Racey**
'Lay Your Love on Me'

7. **Sarah Brightman and Hot Gossip**
'I Lost My Heart to a Starship Trooper'

8. **Rod Stewart**
'Do Ya Think I'm Sexy?'

9. **Chic**
'Le Freak'

10. **Elton John**
'Song for Guy'

leather man Glenn Hughes, Native American Felipe Rose, construction worker David Hodo and military man Alexander Briley.

Meanwhile, at number six, Racey made their Official Chart debut with 'Lay Your Love on Me', co-written by Nicky Chinn and Mike Chapman – the duo responsible for our 1974 Christmas number one.

1979

PINK FLOYD
'ANOTHER BRICK IN THE WALL (PART II)'

WEEKS AT NUMBER ONE 4

FOLLOW-UP SINGLE: 'WHEN THE TIGERS BROKE FREE' AUGUST 1982

HIGHEST CHART POSITION 39

Following two top-forty hits in 1967, Pink Floyd waited twelve years for their next Official Chart entry, with 'Another Brick in the Wall (Part II)' replacing the Police's 'Walking on the Moon' to claim the final Christmas number-one spot of the '70s.

Taken from the band's concept album *The Wall*, which peaked at number three but spent more than a year in the chart, the single's four-week stay at the top was aided by a video featuring animation from cartoonist Gerald Scarfe and a chorus sung by children from Islington Green School. The children were given concert tickets, albums and singles for their time, while the school received a payment of £1,000.

2 February: Sid Vicious, bass player of the Sex Pistols, is found dead in a New York hotel room |

The album and single were both produced by Canadian Bob Ezrin, who also oversaw Alice Cooper's 'School's Out' (1972), Peter Gabriel's 'Solsbury Hill' (1977), Rod Stewart's 'Every Beat of My Heart' (1986) and U2 and Green Day's collaboration 'The Saints Are Coming' (2006) – all of which reached the top twenty.

In July 1990, 'Another Brick' songwriter Roger Waters recorded a live version with singer Cyndi Lauper at Potsdamer Platz in Berlin. The same public square was later immortalised by David Bowie in 'Where Are We Now?' – the final top-forty hit of his lifetime.

NUMBER TWO
ABBA
'I HAVE A DREAM'

It's more likely to happen at Christmas, but there can't be many instances when the number-one and number-two singles both feature a school choir. The addition of the International School of Stockholm Choir to ABBA's seventeenth consecutive top-forty hit did give rise to such an event, though. 'I Have a Dream' was taken from the band's sixth studio album, *Voulez-Vous*, which was itself a number one for four weeks. However, unlike the band's four previous original collections, it failed to yield a number-one single:

1979
CHRISTMAS TOP TEN

1 Pink Floyd
'Another Brick in the Wall (Part II)'

2 ABBA
'I Have a Dream'

3 The Police
'Walking on the Moon'

4 Fiddler's Dram
'Day Trip to Bangor (Didn't We Have a Lovely Time)'

5 The Tourists
'I Only Want to Be with You'

6 Sugarhill Gang
'Rapper's Delight'

7 Paul McCartney
'Wonderful Christmastime'

8 Gibson Brothers
'Que Sera Mi Vida (If You Should Go)'

9 Three Degrees
'My Simple Heart'

10 The Pretenders
'Brass in Pocket'

'Chiquitita' was kept from the top by Blondie's 'Heart of Glass', while 'Does Your Mother Know' peaked at number four. (Impatient readers can skip to 1999 for details of how 'I Have a Dream' eventually became a Christmas number one...)

2 September: Tony Blackburn succeeds Simon Bates as presenter of Radio 1's top-forty show

TAKE IT FROM THE TOP

A timeline charting almost 150 years of the key developments that have shaped how we listen to the Christmas number-one single...

1877

Thomas Edison invents the phonograph – a manual device for recording and playing back sound – using tinfoil wrapped around a cylinder.

Alexander Graham Bell unveils the wind-up Graphophone, which captures sound recordings on a flat disc.

1881

1894

Emile Berliner's first 78-rpm records are issued. The 5-inch or 7-inch discs are made of shellac – a resin secreted by lac bugs.

The first 12-inch 78-rpm records are produced, which play up to five minutes of music on each side.

1903

1908

Deutsche Grammophon release a complete recording of the opera *Carmen* on multiple discs housed in specially designed 'album' packaging.

Victor Talking Machine Company launch the Orthophonic Electrola record player to play electrically amplified discs. It costs $650 at a time when the price of a new Ford Model T car is $300.

1925

1931

British electronics engineer Alan Blumlein files a patent for binaural or stereophonic sound, while RCA Victor introduce vinyl records, though the expensive cost limits their use.

Columbia Records launch the 12-inch 33⅓-rpm vinyl long player – or 'LP'.

1948

1949

RCA Victor launch the 7-inch 45-rpm record, with a single recording on each side.

The *New Musical Express* publishes the very first sales-based UK singles chart – a top twelve. The Dansette record player is also launched – the first model costs the equivalent of £850 in 2021 money.

1952

1958

The BBC begin regular stereo radio broadcasts every Saturday morning.

Dutch company Philips launch the compact cassette tape.

1963

1964

The very first episode of *Top of the Pops* airs on BBC TV.

DJ Tony Blackburn launches BBC Radio 1. The number-one single that week is 'The Last Waltz' by Engelbert Humperdinck.

1967

1973

Motorola demonstrate the first cellular mobile phone, weighing in at 2 kilograms (equivalent to two bags of sugar).

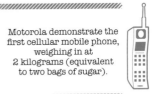

The first 12-inch single is released in the UK.

1976

1979

Sony launch the Walkman portable cassette player.

The first commercially available compact disc (CD) is produced – a recording of Chopin waltzes.

1982

1984

Sony launch the first portable CD player. Dire Straits' 'Brothers in Arms' becomes the UK's first CD single.

Elton John's 'Candle in the Wind 1997' becomes the biggest-selling single of all time in the UK, while Capitol Records' remix of Duran Duran's 'Electric Barbarella' is available as a download.

1997

2001

Apple launch the iTunes Store and the iPod MP3 player.

Gnarls Barkley's 'Crazy' becomes the first single to reach number one from downloads alone. The Official Chart reports that digital tracks now account for 78 per cent of all single sales.

2006

2014

Music-streaming data is added to the Official Chart, with 100 streams equating to the sale or download of one single.

Video streaming joins music streaming in counting towards the Official Chart.

2018

WELCOME TO THE '80s

A new decade and the first new number ones went to new-ish acts – the Pretenders with 'Brass In Pocket', followed by the Specials with *The Special AKA Live!* (EP). Normal service was resumed by May when Johnny Logan's Eurovision-winning 'What's Another Year' was replaced by the ten-year-old theme tune from TV series *M*A*S*H*, 'Suicide Is Painless'.

Chart hits driven by TV adverts weren't exactly new – in 1971, the New Seekers had taken soft-drink jingle 'I'd Like to Teach the World to Sing (In Perfect Harmony)' all the way to number one – but a series of nostalgic denim campaigns in the mid-'80s reintroduced a wave of '60s hits to the Official Chart. 'Wonderful World' by Sam Cooke, 'When a Man Loves a Woman' by Percy Sledge and 'I Heard It Through the Grapevine' by Marvin Gaye all made their way back into the top ten, while Ben E. King's 1961 'Stand by Me' went all the way to number one.

Festivals at Glastonbury, Reading, Knebworth and Donington were now a regular part of the music calendar, though the arrival of acid house and the 'Second Summer of Love' in 1988 saw the introduction of raves, both impromptu and organised, if not entirely legal. However,

the mother of all live events took place on 13 July 1985, with DJ Richard Skinner announcing: 'It's 12 noon in London, 7 a.m. in Philadelphia, and around the world it's time for Live Aid.' Around 162,000 people attended the two main events, while an estimated 1.9 billion watched on TV.

Live Aid was the next step for a famine-relief campaign that began with Band Aid's 'Do They Know It's Christmas?' – the 1984 Christmas number one – but it also marked the point at which charity singles became a common occurrence at the top of the Official Chart. The second half of the decade saw number ones for: charity supergroups the Crowd and USA for Africa; a fundraising cover of 'Dancing in the Street' by David Bowie and Mick Jagger; the first Comic Relief single from Cliff Richard and the Young Ones; Ferry Aid; Gerry Marsden with Paul McCartney, Holly Johnson and the Christians; Band Aid II; and Wet Wet Wet with – let the record books show – Billy Bragg and pianist Cara Tivey.

In November 1987, Radio 1's *Official Chart* show unveiled the UK's 600th number-one single: T'Pau's 'China in Your Hand'. Over the course of the next three weeks, the station played the other 599 chart-toppers, going back to the launch of the Official Chart in 1952. In further 'mature' radio news, a legal ruling that all independent local stations permanently split their AM and FM frequencies resulted in a number of broadcasters creating 'golden oldies' stations on their AM wavebands, with London's Capital Radio reviving BBC's *Pick of the Pops* programme to present past charts.

Industrial action meant *Top of the Pops* disappeared from our TV screens for eleven weeks in 1980, but it returned with balloons, cheerleaders, whooping, hollering and fresh presenter talent. A series of guest co-presenters included Elton John (teaming up with Peter Powell), Russ Abbott (with Mike Read) and Debbie Harry (with John Peel). The '80s also gave us not one but two new *Top of the Pops* theme tunes: first in 1981, when 'Yellow Pearl' – written by Thin Lizzy's Phil Lynott and Ultravox's Midge Ure – replaced CCS's 'Whole Lotta Love', and again in 1986, alongside a new logo, when 'Yellow Pearl' was succeeded by Paul Hardcastle's 'The Wizard'.

Competition for the music TV audience arrived in 1987 from MTV Europe. The launch of the original music video channel in the US six years earlier had prompted the 'Second British Invasion', led by the shiny, happy New Romantic and synth-pop acts. Closer to home, Channel 4 launched *The Tube*, which ran for five series from 1982 to 1987. The first episode featured the last live TV appearance by the Jam, who split after a run of four number-one hits. As well as introducing bands like Frankie Goes to Hollywood and the Proclaimers to the nation, the programme also broadcast exclusive performances by Madonna, Robert Plant, Tina Turner, and ZZ Top.

On BBC Two, performers on the *Oxford Road Show*, which went out between 1981 and 1985, included Duran Duran, Soft Cell, Tears for Fears, UB40, and the Smiths. ITV offered the children's programme *Razzmatazz* between 1981 and 1987, with chances to see Chas and Dave, Madness, Kim Wilde, and Bucks Fizz. Towards the end of the decade, not content with dominating the Official Chart, producer Pete Waterman teamed up with Michaela Strachan to present *The Hitman and Her* – required viewing for weary punters returning from the pubs and clubs who needed one last blast of 2 Unlimited before they fell asleep on the sofa.

The Official Chart itself changed in 1983, allowing dedicated or inquisitive music fans to examine the top 100 singles. Other changes included: banning the use of 'free gifts' that were potentially worth more than the single; limiting the number of formats that would count towards a chart place; and capping the total duration of a single's tracks at twenty minutes (anything longer was considered an album). There was even a brief ban on CDs in the Official Singles Chart, though this was lifted by May 1987 and Whitney Houston's 'I Wanna Dance with Somebody (Who Loves Me)' became the first number one released as a CD single.

That same year, Steve 'Silk' Hurley's 'Jack Your Body' became the first house music track to reach number one, closely followed by the huge-selling 'Pump Up the Volume', courtesy of British act M|A|R|R|S. With disco music a fading memory, the Official Chart said hello to a plethora of new genres, including techno, hi-NRG, Balearic beats, ambient house and Italo house.

Seemingly immune to trends was Madonna, who had her first number one – the 1985 hit 'Into the Groove', taken from the film *Desperately Seeking Susan* – plus a further five chart-toppers before the decade was out. She even doubled up on the Official Chart double – having a number-one single and album in the same week – with both 'Papa Don't Preach'/*True Blue* and 'Like a Prayer'/*Like a Prayer*.

As the '80s drew to a close, Black Box sat at number one with 'Ride on Time', the Official Albums Chart was split in two with the introduction of the Official Compilations Chart, old songs got sampled, bunnys got jiving and there was a school of thought that the dancefloor was where it was at. Surely the charts would belong to the ravers from now on and every Christmas number one would be a million-selling techno, house or trance classic?

Let's find out…

Official Christmas Number 1

1980

ST WINIFRED'S SCHOOL CHOIR
'THERE'S NO ONE QUITE LIKE GRANDMA'

WEEKS AT NUMBER ONE
2

FOLLOW-UP SINGLE: 'HOLD MY HAND'
OCTOBER 1981

HIGHEST CHART POSITION
DID NOT CHART

You wait ages to have a school choir on the Christmas number-one single, then two come along in a row. While the history books will show that the children of this Stockport primary school were another addition to our 'one-hit wonders' category, the choir had actually made an uncredited Official Chart debut two years earlier on 'Matchstalk Men and Matchstalk Cats and Dogs' – a number-one and sole top-forty hit for duo Brian and Michael. The pair crossed paths with the choir once more in 1986 when they wrote and

19 January: The first Official Independent Singles Chart is published | 20 May: Royal charity premiere of

produced 'It's 'Orrible Being In Love (When You're Eight and a Half)' for the St Winifred's 'splinter group' Claire and Friends.

The original chart-topping choir line-up included future actress Sally Lindsay, who played Shelley Unwin in *Coronation Street* for five years, thereby bringing us conveniently to the choir's 1993 line-up, which backed Bill Tarmey (aka *Corrie*'s Jack Duckworth) on a Mike Stock/ Pete Waterman-produced cover of the Barry Manilow song 'One Voice'. Should any readers still doubt the pop credentials of the choir, look no further than their backing-vocal contributions on 'You Can't Keep a Good Man Down' by Kid Creole and the Coconuts and 'Bow Down' by the Housemartins.

NUMBER TWO
JOHN LENNON
'(JUST LIKE) STARTING OVER'

First released at the end of October 1980, '(Just Like) Starting Over' seemingly peaked at number eight before slipping to number twenty-one. However, news of John Lennon's tragic death, aged just forty, in New York on 8 December pushed the single to number one the following week.

The first Official Chart of 1981 saw John's 1975 single 'Imagine' begin

1980
CHRISTMAS TOP TEN

1. **St Winifred's School Choir**
'There's No One Quite Like Grandma'

2. **John Lennon**
'(Just Like) Starting Over'

3. **Jona Lewie**
'Stop the Cavalry'

4. **John & Yoko and the Plastic Ono Band with the Harlem Community Choir**
'Happy Xmas (War Is Over)'

5. **ABBA**
'Super Trouper'

6. **The Police**
'De Do Do Do De Da Da Da'

7. **Adam and the Ants**
'Antmusic'

8. **Madness**
'Embarrassment'

9. **John Lennon**
'Imagine'

10. **Stray Cats**
'Runaway Boys'

a four-week run at the top, with John and Yoko's 'Happy Xmas (War Is Over)' holding the number-two spot for a week. At the beginning of February, 'Woman' became John's third chart-topper, making him the first artist since the Beatles (in 1963) to replace themselves at number one.

Star Wars: Episode V – The Empire Strikes Back at the Odeon Cinema in Leicester Square

1981

HUMAN LEAGUE 'DON'T YOU WANT ME'

FOLLOW-UP SINGLE: 'BEING BOILED' (RE-ISSUE)
JANUARY 1982

**WEEKS AT NUMBER ONE
5**

**HIGHEST CHART POSITION
6**

After a change of line-up that saw founding members Ian Craig-Marsh and Martyn Ware leave to form Heaven 17, the Human League made their Official Chart top-forty debut in May 1981 with 'The Sound of the Crowd', followed by two more hits – 'Love Action (I Believe in Love)' and 'Open Your Heart' – from their number-one album, *Dare*.

Singer Phil Oakey was reluctant to release a fourth single from the album, particularly one he regarded as weak, but agreed to on the condition that initial copies included a free poster. History doesn't record how many posters were printed, though it is unlikely that all 1.15 million buyers who made 'Don't You Want Me' the best-selling single of 1981 got one.

The video, directed by Steve Barron (later responsible for Michael Jackson's 'Billie Jean' and A-ha's

5 January: Mike Read succeeds Dave Lee Travis as presenter of *Radio 1 Breakfast* | 6 June: First issue of

'Take On Me'), was supposed to suggest French arthouse cinema – even though François Truffaut isn't known for making films on a wet night in Slough – and helped the single rise to number one in the US in July 1982.

In 1992, Liverpudlian group the Farm claimed their sixth entry in the top forty with their version of 'Don't You Want Me', which was recorded for the *Ruby Trax* charity compilation album released to celebrate the *NME*'s fortieth birthday. The Human League's original re-entered the Official Chart in 1995 at number sixteen, when it was re-issued in support of a *Greatest Hits* collection, then once more in 2014, when it peaked at number nineteen following a campaign by supporters of Aberdeen FC, who had taken to serenading their team's midfield player to the tune of the chorus ('Peter Pawlett, baby!').

NUMBER TWO
CLIFF RICHARD
'DADDY'S HOME'

For a third time, Cliff held the festive runner-up spot following his 1962 and 1965 results. 'Daddy's Home' actually had a history of peaking at number two, with the original 1961 recording by doo-wop trio Shep and the Limelites playing second fiddle to Ricky Nelson's 'Travellin' Man' in the

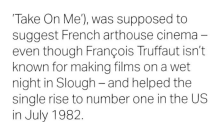

1981
CHRISTMAS TOP TEN

1 Human League
'Don't You Want Me'

2 Cliff Richard
'Daddy's Home'

3 ABBA
'One of Us'

4 Adam and the Ants
'Ant Rap'

5 Bucks Fizz
'The Land of Make Believe'

6 Madness
'It Must Be Love'

7 Godley & Creme
'Wedding Bells'

8 Status Quo
'Rock 'n' Roll'

9 Dollar
'Mirror Mirror (Mon Amour)'

10 Jon and Vangelis
'I'll Find My Way Home'

US. While Cliff's is the only version to chart in the UK, Jermaine Jackson released 'Daddy's Home' as a 1972 solo single, Toots and the Maytals recorded a reggae alternative for their 1973 *Funky Kingston* album and the Carpenters included it in their 'Oldies Medley' on the 1974 *Live in Japan* album.

1982

RENÉE AND RENATO 'SAVE YOUR LOVE'

FOLLOW-UP SINGLE: 'JUST ONE MORE KISS'
FEBRUARY 1983

WEEKS AT NUMBER ONE 4

HIGHEST CHART POSITION 48

Italian-born Renato Pagliari got his showbiz break when he auditioned for the ITV talent show *New Faces* in 1975. (Eventual winner: comedienne Marti Caine. Fourth place: comedian Lenny Henry.) This brought him to the attention of songwriter Johnny Edward, who paired Renato with Hilary 'Renée' Lester to release 'Save Your Love' – a song he co-wrote with his wife, Sue.

After replacing the Jam's farewell single, 'Beat Surrender', at number

one, 'Save Your Love' stayed at the top for four weeks until Phil Collins' 'You Can't Hurry Love' became the first chart-topper of 1983. Renée and Renato join a fairly exclusive clique within our 'one-hit wonders' category: artists whose only top-forty chart entry was a number-one single. (The founding member of the clique was American singer Kitty Kallen, with her 1954 chart-topper 'Little Things Mean a Lot'.)

Johnny Edward was born Johnny Flux and began his career with British rhythm and blues band the Mannish Boys. In 1964, the band recruited seventeen-year-old Davie

10 January: Tommy Vance succeeds Tony Blackburn as host of Radio 1's chart show | 5 November: Live

Jones as their singer – he would change his name the following year to David Bowie. Johnny also changed his surname that year when he began a short-lived career as a DJ with 'pirate' station Radio London. In 1978, he created and voiced the robot Metal Mickey, who had his own television show on ITV between 1980 and 1983. The majority of its episodes were directed by Mickey Dolenz of the Monkees and the show produced a number of spin-off records, including a cover of the Beatles' 1963 Christmas number one, 'I Want to Hold Your Hand'.

NUMBER TWO
SHAKIN' STEVENS
'BLUE CHRISTMAS'

This was another hugely successful year for Shakin' Stevens, beginning in January with the self-written 'Oh Julie', which became his third Official Chart number one. He followed it up with 'Shirley' (number six in April), 'Give Me Your Heart Tonight' (number eleven in September) and 'I'll Be Satisfied' (number ten in November). The last of these had only just left the top forty when the *Special Edition EP* (catalogue number: SHAKY1) entered the chart. It featured three songs recorded live on Shaky's UK tour earlier in the year, along with a cover of 'Blue Christmas'

1982
CHRISTMAS TOP TEN

 1 Renée and Renato
'Save Your Love'

 2 Shakin' Stevens
'Blue Christmas'

 3 David Bowie and Bing Crosby
'Peace on Earth/
Little Drummer Boy'

 4 Culture Club
'Time (Clock of the Heart)'

 5 Madness
'Our House'

 6 Phil Collins
'You Can't Hurry Love'

 7 David Essex
'A Winter's Tale'

 8 Modern Romance
'Best Years of Our Lives'

 9 Lionel Richie
'Truly'

 10 The Jam
'Beat Surrender'

– a 1964 release for Elvis Presley that just missed out on a place in our Christmas top ten of that year when it stalled at number eleven.

Meanwhile, at number five, Madness can be seen making their third consecutive appearance in the Christmas top ten. This was also the year that they scored their only chart-topper, 'House of Fun', which spent two weeks at the summit.

music show *The Tube* begins on Channel 4 | 9 November: Sitcom *The Young Ones* begins on BBC Two

Official Christmas Number 1

1983

FLYING PICKETS 'ONLY YOU'

WEEKS AT NUMBER ONE 5

FOLLOW-UP SINGLE: 'WHEN YOU'RE YOUNG AND IN LOVE' APRIL 1984

HIGHEST CHART POSITION 7

Ending Billy Joel's five-week stay at the top with 'Uptown Girl', the Flying Pickets' a cappella cover of Yazoo's 1982 hit managed what the Essex synth-pop duo couldn't (they had been held in second place by Germany's 1982 Eurovision winner, 'A Little Peace' by Nicole).

The Pickets' website tells us that their version of 'Only You' remains the only a cappella track to stay at number one for more than a week. This is perhaps a nod to the Housemartins' 'Caravan of Love' – our 1986 Christmas number two – or the vocal gymnastics of Bobby

15 June: Historical sitcom *Blackadder* begins on BBC One | **14 September:** Singer and songwriter Amy

McFerrin's 'Don't Worry, Be Happy', which peaked at number two in October 1988, but was kept from the top by Whitney Houston's 'One Moment in Time'.

The Pickets' follow-up single, a cover of the Marvelettes' 'When You're Young and in Love', again improved on the chart peak of the original version: the Motown trio's 1967 release – their only UK Official Chart entry – plateaued at number thirteen. For their next single, the Pickets released a band original, 'So Close', but it failed to live up to its name, stalling at number eighty-eight.

Pickets' founder member David Brett appeared in the 2001 film *Harry Potter and the Philosopher's Stone* as Dedalus Diggle, while Brian Hibbard starred in *Coronation Street* as garage mechanic Doug Murray, *Emmerdale* as Bobby-John Downes and *EastEnders* as care-home manager Henry Mason.

NUMBER TWO
SLADE
'MY OH MY'

Twelve years after their Official Chart debut, Slade landed their twenty-first top-forty hit and, while the pace would slow, they still had another three hit singles to come over the next eight years.

1983
CHRISTMAS TOP TEN

1 Flying Pickets
'Only You'

2 Slade
'My Oh My'

3 Culture Club
'Victims'

4 Paul Young
'Love of the Common People'

5 Status Quo
'Marguerita Time'

6 Thompson Twins
'Hold Me Now'

7 Billy Joel
'Tell Her About It'

8 Kenny Rogers and Dolly Parton
'Islands in the Stream'

9 Tina Turner
'Let's Stay Together'

10 Cliff Richard
'Please Don't Fall in Love'

In 1996, singer Noddy Holder was immortalised as Banger in the animated children's TV programme *Bob the Builder* and, although his role didn't extend to a guest appearance on the 2000 Christmas number one, he did join our rather exclusive 'Christmas number-one stars who have appeared in *Coronation Street*' club that same year when he made a one-off appearance as Stan Potter, joining residents to save the street's cobbles.

Winehouse born | 28 November: The first *NOW That's What I Call Music!* compilation album is released

1984

BAND AID
'DO THEY KNOW IT'S CHRISTMAS?'

WEEKS AT NUMBER ONE 5

FOLLOW-UP SINGLE: 'DO THEY KNOW IT'S CHRISTMAS?' (RE-ENTRY) DECEMBER 1985

HIGHEST CHART POSITION 3

On 25 November 1984, inspired by BBC journalist Michael Buerk's report on famine in Ethiopia, Bob Geldof and Midge Ure assembled the finest talent available at Notting Hill's SARM Studios to record what was then the fastest-selling single in Official Chart history and the biggest-selling single of all time in the UK.

At that time, the thirty-seven performing artists – representing fourteen different groups and four solo acts* – boasted twenty-three number-one singles between them, with Sting and the Police accounting for five, George Michael and Wham! for four and Paul Weller for four from his time with the Jam.

11 January: Radio 1 DJ Mike Read announces he will not play 'Relax' by Frankie Goes to Hollywood due

(*Note for statisticians: Phil Collins and George Michael appear in both categories, having had solo number-one hits by this time as well as hits with Genesis and Wham!, respectively).

'Do They Know It's Christmas?' was released as a 7-inch and 12-inch single on Monday 3 December, outselling the rest of the top forty combined in its first week (both formats could have claimed the top spot in their own right) and ending the two-week run of Frankie Goes to Hollywood's 'The Power of Love' at number one. The single re-charted in 1985, with a new B-side, 'One Year On', providing details of how the money raised had been spent. Co-songwriter Bob also offers us a (somewhat tenuous) link back to the 1979 Christmas number one, on account of his starring role in the film adaptation of Pink Floyd's *The Wall*.

NUMBER TWO
WHAM!
'LAST CHRISTMAS'/ 'EVERYTHING SHE WANTS'

Good things come to those that wait – and so it would prove for Wham!'s eighth single, which hung around for thirty-six years before finally claiming the top spot. In doing so, it broke the record set by Tony Christie's '(Is This the Way to) Amarillo', which waited a mere thirty-

1984
CHRISTMAS TOP TEN

 Band Aid
'Do They Know It's Christmas?'

 Wham!
'Last Christmas'/'Everything She Wants'

 Paul McCartney and the Frog Chorus
'We All Stand Together'

 Toy Dolls
'Nellie the Elephant'

 Madonna
'Like a Virgin'

 Frankie Goes to Hollywood
'The Power of Love'

 Ray Parker Jr
'Ghostbusters'

 Gary Glitter
'Another Rock 'n' Roll Christmas'

 Paul Young
'Everything Must Change'

 Tears for Fears
'Shout'

three years and four months for its own moment at the summit. Before it topped the Official Chart in the first week of 2021, 'Last Christmas' had the slightly sad honour of being the best-selling single in the UK to never get to number one, despite a total of almost 2 million sales. It now hands that crown to 'Moves Like Jagger' by Maroon 5 featuring Christina Aguilera.

WHAT THE BAND AIDERS DID NEXT

What happened when the stars of the 1984 Christmas number-one single (and the second best-selling UK single of all time) went back to their day jobs?

Adam Clayton, Bono
In May 1985, U2 had their fifth top-forty hit with 'The Unforgettable Fire', which reached number six. Singer Bono then made his solo debut when he featured on Clannad's 1986 single 'In a Lifetime'. In 1996, bass player Adam teamed up with bandmate Larry Mullen to reach number seven with 'Theme from *Mission: Impossible*'.

Andy Taylor, John Taylor, Nick Rhodes, Roger Taylor, Simon Le Bon
Duran Duran's 'only' chart activity in 1985 was the James Bond film theme 'A View to a Kill' – a number-two hit in the UK and the band's second chart-topper in the US. The Power Station (John and Andy's side project) also had two 1985 top-forty hits, while Simon, Nick and Roger (recording as Arcadia) reached number seven in November 1985 with 'Election Day'.

Bob Geldof, Johnny Fingers, Pete Briquette, Simon Crowe
The Boomtown Rats' next single, 'A Hold of Me', stalled at number seventy-eight and would be their last appearance in the Official Singles Chart. Singer Bob Geldof launched his solo career in November 1986 with the single 'This Is the World Calling', which reached number twenty-six.

Boy George, Jon Moss
Culture Club interrupted their American tour to participate in Band Aid, though Boy George arrived late and missed the photo session. After eight consecutive top-forty singles, Culture Club had a fallow year in 1985, but returned to the Official Chart in March 1986 with the number-seven hit 'Move Away'.

Chris Cross, Midge Ure
It wasn't until September 1986 that Ultravox were back in the Official Chart with the single 'Same Old Story' – a number thirty-one. Meanwhile, solo Midge managed what his band couldn't: he scored a chart-topping hit in October 1985 with 'If I Was'.

Dennis Thomas, James 'J.T.' Taylor, Robert 'Kool' Bell
One of two American acts on the Band Aid single, New Jersey soul group Kool & the Gang were back in the top forty in February 1985 when 'Misled' charted at number twenty-eight. Bigger things followed in May when 'Cherish' reached number four in the UK and number two in the US.

Francis Rossi, Rick Parfitt
After famously kicking off Live Aid in July 1985 with 'Rockin' All Over the World', Status Quo returned to the Official Chart seventeen months later with 'Rollin' Home' – the band's thirty-first top-forty hit.

Gary Kemp, John Keeble, Martin Kemp, Steve Norman, Tony Hadley
An extensive world tour and a change of record label meant that Spandau Ballet waited until August 1986 to make their Official Chart return. 'Fight for Ourselves' became their fifteenth top-forty hit, peaking at number fifteen.

George Michael
Though 'Last Christmas' played second fiddle to Band Aid, Wham! scored their third

number-one single in November 1985 with 'I'm Your Man'. The duo announced their break-up in 1986, by which time George had already claimed his second solo number one with 'A Different Corner'.

Glenn Gregory, Martin Ware
Following five top-forty hits in the preceding two years, Heaven 17's first single of 1985, '…(And That's No Lie)', stalled at number fifty-two. Seven years later, the Sheffield trio returned to the upper reaches of the Official Chart with 'Temptation (Brothers in Rhythm Remix)', which peaked at number four.

Jody Watley
After eleven top-forty hits, Chicago-born Jody Watley left soul trio Shalamar in 1983. As her first two solo singles, including the 1985 release 'Girls Night Out', failed to chart, fans had to wait until 1987 for her top-forty debut – the number-thirteen hit 'Looking for a New Love'.

Keren Woodward, Sara Dallin, Siobhan Fahey
Bananarama's only Official Chart showing in 1985 was the single 'Do Not Disturb', which reached number thirty-one. The band returned the following year with a Stock Aitken Waterman-produced cover of Shocking Blue's 1969 single 'Venus'. It peaked at number eight in the UK and went all the way to the top in the US.

Marilyn
After three top-forty hits that peaked progressively lower, Marilyn's fourth single, 'Baby U Left Me', stalled at number seventy in April 1985. In 2002, he collaborated with fellow Band Aider Boy George on a non-charting cover version of 'Spirit in the Sky'.

Paul Weller
Paul's band the Style Council had their eighth consecutive top-forty hit in May 1985 when 'Walls Come Tumbling Down' reached number six. In November, Style Council singer Dee C. Lee had her only solo top-forty hit with 'See the Day' – a song covered by Christmas number-one artists Girls Aloud, whose version reached number nine in 2005.

Paul Young
Paul was also in the Christmas top ten in 1984 with 'Everything Must Change'. In 1985, he picked up the Best Male Solo Artist BRIT Award and released a number-four cover of the Daryl Hall and John Oates song 'Everytime You Go Away'.

Phil Collins
While 'Do They Know It's Christmas?' was still in the top ten, Phil had his sixth solo top-forty hit in January 1985 with 'Sussudio', which peaked at number twelve. Genesis took a bit of time out that year, but returned to the top forty in May 1986 when 'Invisible Touch' reached number fifteen.

Sting
In 1985, Sting's second solo hit, 'If You Love Somebody Set Them Free', reached number twenty-six, while the Police received an Outstanding Contribution to Music BRIT Award. The band returned to the top forty in October 1986 with 'Don't Stand So Close to Me '86', which peaked at number twenty-four.

1985

SHAKIN' STEVENS 'MERRY CHRISTMAS EVERYONE'

FOLLOW-UP SINGLE: 'TURNING AWAY'
MARCH 1986

WEEKS AT NUMBER ONE
2

HIGHEST CHART POSITION
15

With the top-three singles from Christmas 1984 all re-entering the chart (Paul McCartney and the Frog Chorus's 'We All Stand Together' at number thirty-two, Wham!'s 'Last Christmas' at number six and Band Aid's 'Do They Know It's Christmas?' at number three), the chart-topping feat of Shaky's 'Merry Christmas Everyone' was a triumph of patience and pragmatism.

Produced by Christmas number-one veteran Dave Edmunds ('I Hear You Knocking', 1970) and written by Bob Heatlie (of Aneka's 'Japanese Boy' fame), the song was ready for release the previous Christmas, but, as Band Aid was heaving into view (without Shaky's participation), Stevens held tight for another twelve months. 'I thought the song deserved to be number one and didn't want to be number two,' he

6 April: Music video programme *The Max Headroom Show* begins on Channel 4 | 21 June: Singer and

remarked over a valedictory eggnog in 1985.

Having toiled unsuccessfully throughout the 1970s alongside his Sunsets, chart success came late for Michael 'Shakin' Stevens' Barratt. Upon striking out alone in 1980, 'Hot Dog' (number twenty-four) was the first of Shaky's thirty-three top-forty singles – including four chart-toppers – over a 25-year period. His 1981 number one 'This Ole House' provides us with a link back to our very first Christmas top ten, which featured Rosemary Clooney: among Rosemary's seven top-forty hits was her own number-one version of 'This Ole House' in 1954. Meanwhile, Shaky's first self-penned chart-topper, 'Oh Julie' (January 1982), was a minor hit in the US for Barry Manilow, thus proving that Barry doesn't actually write all the songs that make the whole world sing.

NUMBER TWO
WHITNEY HOUSTON
'SAVING ALL MY LOVE FOR YOU'

Following her own two-week stint at number one, Whitney spent two weeks behind Shaky over Christmas, followed by a New Year looking up at Pet Shop Boys' 'West End Girls'.

'Saving All My Love for You' was the first of four UK number-one hits

1985
CHRISTMAS TOP TEN

 1 Shakin' Stevens
'Merry Christmas Everyone'

 2 Whitney Houston
'Saving All My Love for You'

 3 Band Aid
'Do They Know It's Christmas?'

 4 Pet Shop Boys
'West End Girls'

 5 Aled Jones
'Walking in the Air'

 6 Wham!
'Last Christmas'/'Everything She Wants'

 7 Phil Collins and Marilyn Martin
'Separate Lives'

 8 Wham!
'I'm Your Man'

 9 Madonna
'Dress You Up'

 10 Dee C. Lee
'See the Day'

for Whitney and the first of seven consecutive number-one singles for her in the US. Fun fact: the smooth sax solo on this single was played by veteran brass honker Tom Scott. Not only was Tom the saxophonist to the stars (with credits including Michael Jackson's 'Billie Jean' and Rod Stewart's 'Do Ya Think I'm Sexy?'), he also wrote the theme tune for TV's *Starsky and Hutch*.

songwriter Lana Del Rey born | 13 July: Live Aid concerts staged in London and Philadelphia

1986

JACKIE WILSON 'REET PETITE (THE SWEETEST GIRL IN TOWN)'

FOLLOW-UP SINGLE: 'I GET THE SWEETEST FEELING' (RE-ENTRY) MARCH 1987

WEEKS AT NUMBER ONE 4

HIGHEST CHART POSITION 3

After an appearance in the 1957 Christmas top ten and a number-six peak the following January, Jackie Wilson's 'Reet Petite' – the first of his nine top-forty hits – was seemingly confined to the history books, with a reference showing that the song's success helped co-writer Berry Gordy fund his fledgling Motown record label.

Almost thirty years later, a screening of an eye-catching 'claymation' video on BBC arts programme *Arena* prompted a re-issue that saw the song knock the Housemartins' 'Caravan of Love' from the top spot, giving Jackie the first posthumous Christmas number one in Official Chart history. (The Hull quartet had reaped the benefits of their own animated video earlier that year when 'Happy Hour' went to number three in June).

28 June: At London's Wembley Stadium, Wham! play their final concert | 25 December: Over 30 million

A namecheck in the title of the 1982 Dexys Midnight Runners hit 'Jackie Wilson Said' (following the mention of Maroon 5 and Christina Aguilera's 'Moves Like Jagger' in our account of Christmas 1984) presents the perfect opportunity to explore top-forty artists who have been immortalised in top-forty hits. We begin in 1977 with 'I Remember Elvis Presley', a number-four (and sole) hit for Danny Mirror, then on to another rock 'n' roll legend, 'Buddy Holly', who Weezer took to number twelve in May 1995. Eulogies to female artists include 'Barbra Streisand' by Duck Sauce, which spent two weeks at number three in 2010, and the Wanted's 2013 number four, 'Walks Like Rihanna'. A prize will be sent to the House of Love for mentioning two number-one acts in their 1990 top-forty single 'Beatles and the Stones'.

NUMBER TWO
THE HOUSEMARTINS
'CARAVAN OF LOVE'

The fourth of the Housemartins' seven top-forty hits and their only Official Chart cover, 'Caravan of Love' was originally recorded by US trio Isley-Jasper-Isley, who – as the name suggests – featured brothers Ernie and Marvin Isley plus brother-in-law Chris Jasper, all previously members of the Isley Brothers.

1986
CHRISTMAS TOP TEN

1. **Jackie Wilson**
'Reet Petite (The Sweetest Girl in Town)'

2. **The Housemartins**
'Caravan of Love'

3. **Europe**
'The Final Countdown'

4. **Madonna**
'Open Your Heart'

5. **Erasure**
'Sometimes'

6. **Oran 'Juice' Jones**
'The Rain'

7. **A-ha**
'Cry Wolf'

8. **Alison Moyet**
'Is This Love?'

9. **Gregory Abbott**
'Shake You Down'

10. **Bon Jovi**
'Livin' on a Prayer'

The Housemartins came within a week of giving us a second a cappella Christmas number one and – although the band never scaled such giddy heights again – their frontman, Paul Heaton, did top the Official Chart in 1990 as part of the Beautiful South, while bass player Norman Cook went to number one in 1999 under the alias Fatboy Slim.

viewers watch Den Watts serve divorce papers to his wife, Angie, on TV soap *EastEnders*

Official Christmas Number 1

1987

PET SHOP BOYS 'ALWAYS ON MY MIND'

WEEKS AT NUMBER ONE
5

FOLLOW-UP SINGLE: 'HEART'
APRIL 1988

HIGHEST CHART POSITION
1

After abandoning plans to record a house version of Elvis Presley's 1955 single 'Baby Let's Play House', Pet Shop Boys landed their third of four number ones with their cover of 'Always on My Mind', recorded for a TV special marking the tenth anniversary of the death of 'The King' (our Christmas number-one artist in 1962). The programme, *Love Me Tender*, also featured Kim Wilde (another artist from this year's top ten), Boy George (Christmas number one with Band Aid in 1984) and Dave Edmunds (Christmas number one in 1970).

9 June: Music show *The Roxy* begins on ITV, presented by David 'Kid' Jensen and Kevin Sharkey |

Pet Shop Boys had originally planned to make 'Always on My Mind' available as the B-side of their number-eight hit 'Rent' (and, in Japan, a demo recording of the song was given away with initial copies of *Actually*, their second album). However, when common sense prevailed, not only did 'Always on My Mind' replace Rick Astley's cover of 'When I Fall in Love' at number one, it also became the fourteenth best-selling single of 1987 and helped the band win Best British Group at the 1988 BRIT Awards. At the ceremony, the duo performed 'What Have I Done to Deserve This?' with Dusty Springfield, who first graced our story in 1963 when 'I Only Want to Be with You' sat at number five in the Christmas top ten.

NUMBER TWO
THE POGUES FEAT. KIRSTY MacCOLL
'FAIRYTALE OF NEW YORK'

The Pogues had planned to record 'Fairytale of New York' for their 1986 top-forty debut, *Poguetry in Motion* (EP), with the female vocal part sung by bassist Cait O'Riordan – the then-wife of their producer, Elvis Costello. However, the band didn't record a version they deemed worthy of release until they worked with a new producer, Steve Lilywhite, whose

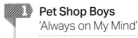

1987
CHRISTMAS TOP TEN

1 Pet Shop Boys
'Always on My Mind'

2 The Pogues feat. Kirsty MacColl
'Fairytale of New York'

3 Mel & Kim
'Rockin' Around the Christmas Tree'

4 Rick Astley
'When I Fall in Love'

5 Alison Moyet
'Love Letters'

6 Michael Jackson
'The Way You Make Me Feel'

7 Nat 'King' Cole
'When I Fall in Love'

8 Belinda Carlisle
'Heaven Is a Place on Earth'

9 T'Pau
'China in Your Hand'

10 Shakin' Stevens
'What Do You Want to Make Those Eyes at Me For?'

wife, Kirsty MacColl, took on the female lead.

'Fairytale of New York' has returned to the top forty every year since 2005 (when it reached number three). The proceeds from its sales that year were donated to homeless charities and to a campaign to investigate Kirsty's tragic death in 2000.

4 October: The Official Singles Chart moves from Tuesday lunchtime to a new Sunday afternoon slot

1988

CLIFF RICHARD 'MISTLETOE AND WINE'

WEEKS AT NUMBER ONE 4

FOLLOW-UP SINGLE: 'THE BEST OF ME' JUNE 1989

HIGHEST CHART POSITION 2

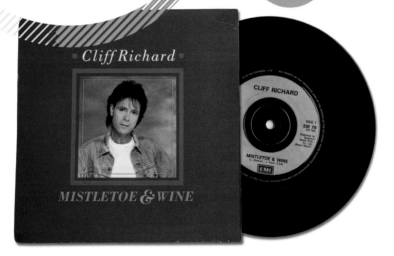

Twenty-nine years after his first Official Chart number-one single and thirty years after his first appearance in the Christmas top ten, Cliff's twelfth number one was also his second festive chart-topper, following a gap of twenty-eight years.

'Mistletoe and Wine' has its roots in the 1976 stage musical *Scraps*, an adaptation of Hans Christian Andersen's story 'The Little Match Girl', first published in 1845. When the musical was filmed for television, 'Mistletoe and Wine' was sung by Twiggy. Incidentally, Twiggy's only Official Chart entry, 'Here I Go Again', reached number seventeen in 1976, just a month after 'I Can't Ask for Anymore

15 February: Sci-fi comedy *Red Dwarf* begins on BBC Two | 23 May: Simon Mayo succeeds Mike Smith

Than You' – Cliff's sixty-seventh consecutive top-forty single – had reached number seventeen.

After it knocked 'The First Time' by Robin Beck from the top spot on 4 December, 'Mistletoe and Wine' became the best-selling single of 1990, though co-writer Keith Strachan – who had previously offered the song to Dennis Waterman and to Val Doonican – said the royalties paid for 'a holiday, but not a house'. However, former maths teacher Keith had more luck in 1998 when he and son Matthew wrote the theme tune for *Who Wants to Be a Millionaire?*. The TV quiz show has run for more than 600 episodes and has been franchised to over 150 countries, making both Strachans millionaires in the process.

NUMBER TWO
KYLIE AND JASON 'ESPECIALLY FOR YOU'

Kylie Minogue's second and Jason Donovan's first number one spent four weeks at number two before it rose to the top for three weeks in January 1989, riding on the euphoria generated by the couple's on-screen wedding as Charlene Mitchell and Scott Robinson in Australian soap *Neighbours*. Further evidence of this excitement can be witnessed at number four in the Christmas top ten: Angry Anderson, of rock band

1988
CHRISTMAS TOP TEN

1 **Cliff Richard**
'Mistletoe and Wine'

2 **Kylie and Jason**
'Especially for You'

3 **Erasure**
Crackers International (EP)

4 **Angry Anderson**
'Suddenly'

5 **Status Quo**
'Burning Bridges (On and Off and On Again)'

6 **Inner City**
'Good Life'

7 **Neneh Cherry**
'Buffalo Stance'

8 **Bros**
'Cat Among the Pigeons'/ 'Silent Night'

9 **Four Tops**
'Loco in Acapulco'

10 **Phil Collins**
'Two Hearts'

Rose Tattoo, had his only hit with the ballad 'Suddenly' – the soundtrack to Charlene and Scott's TV nuptials.

In 2001, 8 million viewers tuned in to watch Kylie's TV special, *An Audience With...*, on which she sang 'Especially for You' with Kermit the Frog. This version was never released as a single, so failed to add to the Muppets' three top-forty hits to date.

as presenter of *Radio 1 Breakfast* | 6 December: Singer and songwriter Roy Orbison dies, aged fifty-two

1989

BAND AID II
'DO THEY KNOW IT'S CHRISTMAS?'

In November 1989, the now-ennobled Sir Bob Geldof called on the hugely successful production and songwriting trio Mike Stock, Matt Aitken and Pete Waterman for a first update of 'Do They Know It's Christmas?', resulting in the final number one of the decade.

Stock Aitken Waterman secured their first chart-topper in March 1985 – with Dead or Alive's 'You Spin Me Round (Like a Record)' –

and also oversaw the number-one charity projects by Ferry Aid ('Let It Be', April 1987) and Gerry Marsden, Paul McCartney, Holly Johnson and the Christians ('Ferry Cross the Mersey', 1989).

The Band Aid line-up that gathered at the Hit Factory studio on Sunday 3 December 1989 had twenty-seven Official Chart number ones between them – four more than the original 1984 cast – with Cliff Richard

23 June: Tim Burton's film version of *Batman*, starring Michael Keaton and Jack Nicholson, is released |

accounting for twelve and pop's hottest properties Kylie Minogue and Jason Donovan contributing three each (if we credit them one each for 'Especially for You').

Bananarama's Keren Woodward and Sara Dallin reprised their roles in the chorus, while Luke Goss filled Phil Collins' drum stool, former 10cc drummer Kevin Godley directed the video and Chris Rea added guitar. Also listed on the credits – among Big Fun, D Mob, the Pasadenas, and Wet Wet Wet – were popular Belgian spelling error Technotronics (sic), presumably represented by singer Ya Kid K rather than lip-synching model Felly (initially credited as singer on the group's Official Chart debut, 'Pump Up the Jam').

NUMBER TWO
JIVE BUNNY AND THE MASTERMIXERS
'LET'S PARTY'

Almost as popular as Kylie and Jason in 1989 was cartoon rabbit Jive Bunny, whose three number-one singles spent a combined total of nine weeks at the top between August and December. The novelty act's run began with 'Swing the Mood' – a medley of fifteen big band and rock 'n' roll hits. It was the second best-selling record of the year and reached number eleven in the US.

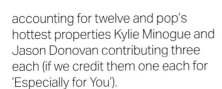

1989
CHRISTMAS TOP TEN

1. **Band Aid II**
   'Do They Know It's Christmas?'

2. **Jive Bunny and the Mastermixers**
   'Let's Party'

3. **Jason Donovan**
   'When You Come Back to Me'

4. **Andy Stewart**
   'Donald Where's Your Troosers?'

5. **Madonna**
   'Dear Jessie'

6. **Soul II Soul**
   'Get a Life'

7. **Kaoma**
   'Lambada'

8. **Tina Turner**
   'I Don't Wanna Lose You'

9. **Linda Ronstadt and Aaron Neville**
   'Don't Know Much'

10. **Bros**
    'Sister'

'That's What I Like' repeated the formula with twelve different rock 'n' roll hits, before festive-themed 'Let's Party' made Jive Bunny and the Mastermixers only the third act ever to reach number one with their first three singles, following on from Gerry and the Pacemakers in 1964 and Frankie Goes to Hollywood in 1984.

10 July: Music magazine programme *The O-Zone* begins on BBC One

MANY HAPPY CHRISTMAS RETURNS

PART II

Jethro Tull
'Ring Out, Solstice Bells'
First top-forty peak: 28 (1976)
This was one of seven top-forty hits for the Tull – a run that includes their 1969 number three, 'Living in the Past', but sadly doesn't feature the 1989 single 'Another Christmas Song', which only managed two weeks at number ninety-five.

Bing Crosby
'White Christmas'
First top-forty peak: 5 (1977)
First recorded by Bing in the pre-Official Chart days of 1942, 'White Christmas' is estimated to have sold more than 50 million copies, so it is still a shock to discover that it didn't chart until December 1977.

Paul McCartney
'Wonderful Christmastime'
First top-forty peak: 6 (1979)
Paul's 'wonderful' hit has returned to the top-forty every year since 2016, though the age of streaming has yet to embrace the joys of its original B-side, the violin-led instrumental 'Rudolph The Red-Nosed Reggae'.

Jona Lewie
'Stop the Cavalry'
First top-forty peak: 3 (1980)
This was one of just two top-forty hits for Jona, along with the 1980 number sixteen 'You'll Always Find Me in the Kitchen at Parties'. Jona was previously a member of Terry Dactyl and the Dinosaurs, whose 1972 number-two single, 'Sea Side Shuffle', was kept from the top by Alice Cooper's 'School's Out'.

Kate Bush
'December Will Be Magic Again'
First top-forty peak: 29 (1980)
First unleashed by Kate as part of her 1979 BBC TV special, this song wasn't released as a single until eleven months later. Fans ignored the month-specific title and kept it in the top forty until the middle of January 1981.

David Bowie and Bing Crosby
'Peace on Earth/Little Drummer Boy'
First top-forty peak: 3 (1982)
Recorded just five weeks before Bing's death in October 1977, this collaboration between Bing (aged seventy-four) and David (aged thirty-one) was part of the TV special *Bing Crosby's Merrie Olde Christmas.*

The Waitresses
'Christmas Wrapping'
First top-forty peak: N/A
Having only peaked at number forty-five, this 1982 release has surprisingly never been a top-forty hit for Ohio band the Waitresses, even though it has returned to the lower reaches of the Official Chart five times and has been covered by both Kylie Minogue and the Spice Girls.

David Essex
'A Winter's Tale'
First top-forty peak: 2 (1983)
Written by the Wombles' Mike Batt and musical maestro Tim Rice, this single – not to be confused with Queen's 1995 number six of the same name – spent a week at number two behind 'You Can't Hurry Love' by Phil Collins.

The Pretenders
'2000 Miles'
First top-forty peak: 15 (1983)
Another festive favourite that has made several attempts to get back into the top forty, this single only managed number sixty-one at the end of 2019 (its best effort since its original peak), though it has been covered by Coldplay, Kylie Minogue (again) and KT Tunstall.

Aled Jones
'Walking in the Air'
First top-forty peak: 5 (1985)
The theme song for the animated film of Raymond Briggs' *The Snowman*, this single was recorded by the then-fourteen-year-old Aled, whose only other top-forty hit was 'Silver Bells' – a Christmas duet with radio colossus Terry Wogan.

Bruce Springsteen
'Santa Claus Is Comin' to Town'
First top-forty peak: 9 (1985)
This version returned to the Official Chart at number forty-eight in 2017, while the 1972 version by the Jackson 5, which originally peaked at number forty-three, cracked the top forty in 2018, charting at number thirty. A version by the Carpenters reached number thirty-seven in 1975.

Chris de Burgh
'A Spaceman Came Travelling'
First top-forty peak: 40 (1986)
A top-forty hit by the narrowest of margins, namely one week at number forty, this single includes squiggly synthesiser noises by David Hentschel, who supplied the same service on Elton John's 1972 number two, 'Rocket Man'.

Mel & Kim
'Rockin' Around the Christmas Tree'
First top-forty peak: 3 (1987)
This version by Mel Smith and Kim Wilde, who are not to be confused with the 'respectable' chart-topping duo Mel and Kim, was recorded as a Comic Relief single in 1987. In 2020, Justin Bieber's version of the song took him to number four, while Brenda Lee's 1962 original has returned her to the top forty another five times.

Saint Etienne
'I Was Born on Christmas Day'
First top-forty peak: 37 (1993)
Regular singer Sarah Cracknell (born on an April day) was joined by guest vocalist Tim Burgess of the Charlatans (born on a May day) for this possible homage to the band's Bob Stanley, who, like Annie Lennox of Eurythmics and Shane MacGowan of the Pogues, really was born on...

WELCOME TO THE '90s

When the first chart-topper of the decade went to New Kids on the Block's 'Hangin' Tough', it heralded an era rich with boy bands and girl groups who would play a significant part in the contest for Christmas number one. These bands and groups would also be the springboard for several successful solo careers, though the beautiful, eclectic nature of the Official Chart would still find room for comedy songs, football songs, charity songs, TV spin-offs, film spin-offs, dance tunes, reggae, ragga and rave.

Putting aside genres, the '90s saw a trend for longer hits, as exemplified by Oasis's 1998 number one, 'All Around the World', which clocked in at nine minutes and thirty-eight seconds, or Bon Jovi's 1994 number nine, 'Dry County', at nine minutes and fifty-two seconds. Meat Loaf, though not known for the brevity of his songs, resisted unleashing the full twelve-minute album version of 'I'd Do Anything for Love (But I Won't Do That)', opting for a more digestible seven minutes and forty-eight seconds for the video and a radio-friendly edit of five minutes and thirteen seconds. It was the Orb who took home the decade's 'long song' trophy, however, with a mix of their 1992 number eight, 'Blue Room', coming in at 39 minutes and 58 seconds.

On the heels of Kylie and Jason, the road from soap to pop looked much busier, with the pair's *Neighbours* co-stars Craig McLachlan and Natalie Imbruglia both scoring number-two hits with their respective chart debuts, 'Mona' and 'Torn'. From *Home and Away*, Kylie's sister Dannii Minogue racked up twelve top-forty hits and even went mononymous (or Minogue-less) for a spell, beginning with the 1997 number four 'All I Wanna Do'.

Closer to home (if you live near Walford or Weatherfield), *EastEnders*' Sean 'Adrian Brosnan' Maguire had an impressive eight top-forty hits, while *Coronation Street* gave us Adam 'Nick Tilsley' Rickitt with three, Bill 'Jack Duckworth' Tarmey with two and Matthew 'Chris Collins' Marsden, who somehow persuaded Destiny's Child to appear on his 1998 cover of Hall & Oates's 'She's Gone'.

However, the biggest success was had by Robson Green and Jerome Flynn, from the ITV drama *Soldier Soldier*, who managed to squeeze six double A-side covers into three number-one spots, becoming the third act to take 'Unchained Melody' to the top (after Jimmy Young and the Righteous Brothers), the second with 'I Believe' (after our 1953 Christmas number-one artist Frankie Laine) and the first with 'What Becomes of the Brokenhearted' (Jimmy Ruffin's original peaked at number four when it was re-issued in 1974).

TV programmes featuring actual musicians included the prime-time BBC Two magazine show *The O-Zone*, a mixture of interviews, live performances and videos, which lasted throughout the '90s. In the first half of the decade, Channel 4 offered us *The Word*, which courted controversy for its unsavoury viewer antics but also gave national television debuts to Nirvana and Oasis. In a similar vein was *The Girlie Show*, a snapshot of 'ladette' culture and the first TV programme to feature the Spice Girls. Between them came *The White Room*, which ran from 1995 to 1996 – perfect timing to capture the good and the great of Britpop.

Top of the Pops tried to maintain its premium position with the introduction of the 'retro' *Top of the Pops 2,* a move from Thursday to Friday evening, new logos, new graphics and three new theme tunes, ultimately settling on a revamped 'Whole Lotta Love', which had served them so well in the '70s. With *The Old Grey Whistle Test* put out to grass in 1988, the gap for something a little more mature was filled by *Later ... with Jools Holland*, on which the former Squeeze keyboard player showcased both new and established acts. It also spawned the annual New Year's Eve *Hootenanny* and a series of specials devoting a whole episode to one artist – in the '90s, featured artists included Alice in Chains, Paul Weller, Metallica, R.E.M. and the Verve. The decade was rounded off by the arrival of S Club 7, who first came to public attention in 1999 when they starred in their own television series, *Miami 7*, and claimed the first of four number ones before the year was out.

Key live events included the 1992 Freddie Mercury Tribute Concert for AIDS Awareness, held at London's Wembley Stadium. The death of the Queen frontman the previous year sparked a huge upturn in the band's Official Chart activity, with *Five Live* (EP) – on which the remaining band members were joined by George Michael and Lisa Stansfield – reaching number one in 1993. In 1996, 2.5 million people applied for tickets to see Oasis perform two dates in the grounds of Knebworth House, Hertfordshire – the site of Queen's last show with Freddie Mercury ten years previously. With capacity set at 125,000, the band could have sold out twenty nights.

The impact of film on the Official Chart was particularly notable this decade. In 1991, *Robin Hood: Prince of Thieves* gave us Bryan Adams' '(Everything I Do) I Do It for You', which racked up sixteen consecutive weeks at number one (breaking the eleven-week 1955 record set by Slim Whitman's 'Rose Marie') and is the biggest-selling cassette single of all time. In 1992, the biggest-selling single – taken from the film *The Bodyguard* – was Whitney Houston's cover of 'I Will Always Love You', which spent ten weeks at number one (turn to Christmas 1992 for the full story). Then, in 1994, romantic comedy *Four Weddings and a Funeral* helped the band formerly known as Vortex Motion claim their third number one, with 'Love Is All Around' keeping Wet Wet Wet at the top for fifteen weeks.

Honourable cinematic mentions also go to: Cher's 'The Shoop Shoop Song' from *Mermaids* (five weeks at number one); Partners in Kryme's 'Turtle Power' from *Teenage Mutant Ninja Turtles* (four weeks); Maria McKee's 'Show Me Heaven' from *Days of Thunder* (four weeks); a re-issue of the Righteous Brothers' 'Unchained Melody' from *Ghost* (four weeks); and Celine Dion's 'My Heart Will Go On' from *Titanic* (two weeks).

As the millennium drew to a close, Westlife proclaimed 'I Have a Dream', the first MP3 players went on sale around the same time that 'No Matter What' by Boyzone held the top spot, dance routines and marketing campaigns got slicker and there was a school of thought that pop ballads were where it was at. Surely the charts would belong to fresh-faced boys and girls from now on and every Christmas number one would involve close harmonies, coordinated rising from stools and rousing key changes?

Let's find out...

Official Christmas Number 1

1990

CLIFF RICHARD 'SAVIOUR'S DAY'

FOLLOW-UP SINGLE: 'MORE TO LIFE' SEPTEMBER 1991

WEEKS AT NUMBER ONE 1

HIGHEST CHART POSITION 23

Just when you thought Cliff's extraordinary career couldn't generate any more unique statistics, his thirteenth number-one single gave him his 100th top-forty hit and saw him become the only artist to top the Official Chart in five consecutive decades.

'Saviour's Day' was written by Chris Eaton – the man responsible for 'Little Town', Cliff's 1982 Yuletide number eleven that narrowly

deprived him of yet another listing in this book – and was succeeded at number one by 'Bring Your Daughter … to the Slaughter', Iron Maiden's only chart-topper, thus emphasising the always-eclectic nature of the Official Chart.

Cliff's first number one, 'Living Doll', also credited the Drifters – the original name for the Shadows, who got equal billing on his second chart-topper, 'Travellin' Light'. Since

29 April: Stephen Hendry, aged twenty-one, becomes the youngest world snooker champion ever | 7 July:

then, Cliff's top-forty hits have featured a wide variety of musical partners, beginning with Shadows guitarist Hank Marvin in 1969, Olivia Newton-John in 1980 and 1995, Phil Everly in 1983 and 1994, the London Philharmonic Orchestra in 1983, the cast of *The Young Ones* and Sarah Brightman (separately) in 1986, Van Morrison in 1989, actress Helen Hobson in 1996, and a 2006 re-recording of 'Move It' featuring Queen's Brian May and the Shadows' Brian Bennett. However, the record-buying public were less enthused about 'Slow Rivers', his 1986 duet with Elton John, which peaked at number forty-four, or 'Two to the Power of Love', a 1984 duet with Janet Jackson, which reached number eighty-three.

NUMBER TWO
VANILLA ICE
'ICE ICE BABY'

With a bassline sampled from the 1981 chart-topper 'Under Pressure' by Queen and David Bowie, 'Ice Ice Baby' gave the American rapper born Robert Van Winkle a UK number one on his first attempt, spending four weeks at the top before being relegated to the runner-up spot by Cliff. The success of this single and its number-ten follow-up, 'Play That Funky Music' (a cover of Wild Cherry's 1976 number seven), saw Vanilla Ice

star in romantic comedy *Cool as Ice*, earning him the 1992 Golden Raspberry Award for Worst New Actor. In 2010, 'Under Pressure (Ice Ice Baby)' – a collaboration between Vanilla Ice and *The X Factor* duo Jedward – was kept from the top spot by Owl City's 'Fireflies'.

CHRISTMAS TOP TEN

 Cliff Richard
'Saviour's Day'

 Vanilla Ice
'Ice Ice Baby'

 Righteous Brothers
'You've Lost That Lovin' Feelin''

 Enigma
'Sadeness (Part I)'

 John Travolta and Olivia Newton-John
'The Grease Megamix'

 The Farm
'All Together Now'

 Madonna
'Justify My Love'

 Snap!
'Mary Had a Little Boy'

 MC Hammer
'Pray'

 EMF
'Unbelievable'

Official Christmas Number 1

1991

QUEEN
'BOHEMIAN RHAPSODY'/ 'THESE ARE THE DAYS OF OUR LIVES'

FOLLOW-UP SINGLE:
FIVE LIVE (EP)
MAY 1993

WEEKS AT NUMBER ONE
5

HIGHEST CHART POSITION
1

An outpouring of emotion following the death of Freddie Mercury on 24 November 1991 saw Queen's *Greatest Hits II* return to the top of the Official Albums Chart, while a re-issue of their biggest single, 'Bohemian Rhapsody', went straight to number one on 15 December. This was the third time Queen accomplished the chart double.

'Bohemian Rhapsody' remained at the top until the middle of January

– just as its original release had done in 1975–76. In the process, it became the first record to leave the Official Chart and then return to number one with exactly the same version. (This next occurred in January 2002 when George Harrison's 1971 number one, 'My Sweet Lord', reclaimed the top spot following his death.)

Because both of its stints at the top bridged the New Year, 'Bohemian

11 January: *The Essential Selection*, presented by DJ Pete Tong, makes its debut on Radio 1 |

Rhapsody' is the only record to have been number one in four different years. It is also the third best-selling single of all time, with sales now totalling over 2.6 million, while Queen's 1981 *Greatest Hits* collection is the all-time best-selling album, boasting sales in excess of 6 million.

Elsewhere in the 1991 Christmas chart, Queen's previous single, 'The Show Must Go On', edged back into the top forty, having peaked at number sixteen in October, and Brian May claimed the first of five solo hits with 'Driven by You'.

NUMBER TWO
DIANA ROSS
'WHEN YOU TELL ME THAT YOU LOVE ME'

After twenty-one top-forty hits with the Supremes (including the Motown label's first UK number one, 1964's 'Baby Love'), Diana charted forty-seven times as a solo artist between 1970 and 2005. Among her many hits were two number ones: 'I'm Still Waiting' in 1971 and 'Chain Reaction' in 1986.

'When You Tell Me That You Love Me' was co-written by Albert Hammond (responsible for Aswad's 1988 number one, 'Don't Turn Around') and John Bettis (who had a hand in Madonna's 1985

1991
CHRISTMAS TOP TEN

1 **Queen**
'Bohemian Rhapsody'/'These Are the Days of Our Lives'

2 **Diana Ross**
'When You Tell Me That You Love Me'

3 **George Michael and Elton John**
'Don't Let the Sun Go Down on Me'

4 **KLF feat. Tammy Wynette**
'Justified & Ancient'

5 **Right Said Fred**
'Don't Talk Just Kiss'

6 **Guns N' Roses**
'Live and Let Die'

7 **Kym Sims**
'Too Blind to See It'

8 **Brian May**
'Driven by You'

9 **Hammer**
'Addams Groove'

10 **Shaft**
'Roobarb and Custard'

number two 'Crazy for You'). A 2005 version of 'When You Tell Me That You Love Me' is also Diana's most recent top-forty hit – her collaboration with Westlife peaked at number two, but was kept from the top by Nizlopi with 'JCB Song'. (More on them later...)

14 January: American sitcom *The Fresh Prince of Bel-Air* makes its UK TV debut on BBC Two

Official Christmas Number 1

1992

WHITNEY HOUSTON 'I WILL ALWAYS LOVE YOU'

FOLLOW-UP SINGLE: 'I'M EVERY WOMAN' FEBRUARY 1993

WEEKS AT NUMBER ONE 10

HIGHEST CHART POSITION 4

Spending ten weeks at the top of the Official Chart, 'I Will Always Love You' boasts the longest continuous number-one stay of all our Christmas chart-toppers, though two spells of nine and then five weeks hand 'Bohemian Rhapsody' the title of most weeks in total. An honourable mention goes to 'Do They Know It's Christmas?', with three different versions of the single achieving a combined twelve weeks at number one.

For twenty-seven years, Whitney could also boast the longest run at the top for a female artist, though she was equalled by Rihanna with 'Umbrella' in 2007 and finally beaten in 2019 by Australian singer-songwriter Tones and I, whose single 'Dance Monkey' lasted eleven weeks. 'I Will Always Love You' also marked the first time in forty years that the same song was Christmas number one on both the UK Official Chart and the US Billboard Hot 100, though Whitney managed an even more impressive fourteen weeks at the top in the States.

18 August: Future Spice Girl Emma Bunton appears in BBC soap *EastEnders* as a mugger | 8 September:

While Whitney's recording of the song is the most successful, it could have been one of Elvis Presley's best-known standards had things been different. After taking her original version to number one on the US Hot Country Songs chart in 1974, Dolly Parton was approached by Elvis's manager, Colonel Tom Parker, with an offer for 'The King' to record 'I Will Always Love You', provided he was given half the songwriting rights. Dolly reported it was a difficult offer to decline, but Whitney's version made her 'enough money to buy Graceland'.

NUMBER TWO
MICHAEL JACKSON
'HEAL THE WORLD'

One of fifty-six top-forty hits for Michael in the UK, adding another eleven weeks to his total of almost 450, 'Heal the World' couldn't quite contribute an eighth number one to Michael's overall tally as it was unlucky enough to go up against the best-selling single of the year.

The sixth release from his chart-topping album *Dangerous*, it was supported by a video directed by Joe Pytka – also responsible for the animation/live-action film *Space Jam* in 1996. Along with 'Cry' from 2001, this is just one of two videos made in Michael's

lifetime that feature no footage of the singer himself, though he does appear in only the final fifteen seconds of the video for his 1989 single 'Liberian Girl'.

Cover versions of 'Heal the World' include a 1999 recording by Welsh singer Aled Jones, who appeared at number five in our 1985 Christmas chart with 'Walking in the Air'.

1992
CHRISTMAS TOP TEN

1. **Whitney Houston**
'I Will Always Love You'

2. **Michael Jackson**
'Heal the World'

3. **Charles & Eddie**
'Would I Lie to You?'

4. **Take That**
'Could It Be Magic'

5. **The Shamen**
'Phorever People'

6. **WWF Superstars**
'Slam Jam'

7. **Boney M.**
'Megamix'

8. **Gloria Estefan**
'Miami Hit Mix'

9. **Rod Stewart**
'Tom Traubert's Blues (Waltzing Matilda)'

10. **Madonna**
'Deeper and Deeper'

Primal Scream's *Screamadelica* album wins the first Mercury Music Prize

Official Christmas Number 1

1993

MR BLOBBY
'MR BLOBBY'

WEEKS AT NUMBER ONE
3

FOLLOW-UP SINGLE: 'CHRISTMAS IN BLOBBYLAND'
DECEMBER 1995

HIGHEST CHART POSITION
36

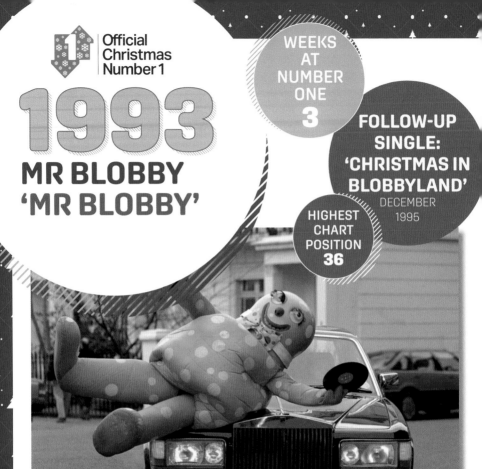

FBM 268

When 'Mr Blobby' by Mr Blobby went to number one on 5 December 1993, it was the first time an eponymous song had achieved this feat in forty-one years of Official Chart history. (Within four months, Dutch duo Doop would become the second act to do so, with their only top-forty hit, 'Doop'.)

'Mr Blobby' looked set to miss out on the Christmas top spot when, after one week, it was displaced by Take That's third chart-topper, 'Babe'. However, the single's irresistible combination of Christmas bells, a children's chorus and a hilarious video – complete with a cameo appearance from Jeremy Clarkson

20 January: Inauguration of Bill Clinton as forty-second president of the US | 3 September: Mark Goodier

(of *Top Gear* notoriety) as Mr Blobby's chauffeur – returned it to the top for a further two weeks and saw it finish the year as the sixth best-selling single of 1993.

A large percentage of Mr Blobby's fanbase must have deserted him by the time of his 1995 follow-up, 'Christmas in Blobbyland' (taken from *Blobby: The Album*), as the single got no higher than number thirty-six. That said, Mr Blobby did make a return (of sorts) to the number-one spot when he appeared in the 2005 video for '(Is This the Way to) Amarillo' – a fundraising release in aid of Comic Relief, credited to Tony Christie featuring Peter Kay.

NUMBER TWO
TAKE THAT
'BABE'

'Babe' was the third of four consecutive number ones from *Everything Changes*, Take That's second album, though it was the only one to spend just a single week at the top. While there is a common thread of Christmas number twos replacing more festive-themed titles at the top when the decorations come down, Take That had to settle for a third week in second place when 'Twist and Shout' by Chaka Demus & Pliers, featuring Jack Radics and

1993
CHRISTMAS TOP TEN

1 **Mr Blobby**
'Mr Blobby'

2 **Take That**
'Babe'

3 **Chaka Demus & Pliers feat. Jack Radics and Taxi Gang**
'Twist and Shout'

4 **Bee Gees**
'For Whom the Bell Tolls'

5 **East 17**
'It's Alright'

6 **Meat Loaf**
'I'd Do Anything for Love (But I Won't Do That)'

7 **Dina Carroll**
'The Perfect Year'

8 **Meat Loaf**
'Bat Out of Hell'

9 **Elton John and Kiki Dee**
'True Love'

10 **Frankie Goes to Hollywood**
'The Power of Love'

Taxi Gang, overtook them in the first chart of 1994. Incidentally, the Beatles' 1963 recording of 'Twist and Shout' missed out on a place in the Official Singles Chart because it was released as part of a four-song EP, but it did spend ten weeks at number one on the Official EP Chart (a separate list that ran between March 1960 and December 1967).

succeeds Simon Mayo as presenter of *Radio 1 Breakfast*

1994

EAST 17
'STAY ANOTHER DAY'

FOLLOW-UP SINGLE: 'LET IT RAIN'
MARCH 1995

WEEKS AT NUMBER ONE
5

HIGHEST CHART POSITION
10

The tenth of (appropriately) seventeen top-forty hits for the postcode pop stars, 'Stay Another Day' would be the group's only number one. Though the heartfelt ballad fails to mention Christmas, the boys did don white parkas in the snow for its video and the peal of bells ramps up the Yuletide bonhomie.

The four-track CD single also included: an up-tempo 'Less SAD Mix', which paired the poignant lyrics of the original song with a bangin' dance beat; a 'More SAD Mix', which added the noise of barking dogs and seagulls; and a 'Not So SAD Mix', because nothing says 'Christmas' quite like a trance anthem. It was nominated for British Single of the Year at the BRIT Awards the following February, but, in the heady days of Britpop, almost inevitably lost out to Blur.

29 May: 'Love Is All Around' by Wet Wet Wet begins a fifteen-week run at the top of the Official

In 2002, the song was covered by Girls Aloud on the CD single for their own Christmas number one, 'Sound of the Underground', though an instrumental version they included on some formats may have left a few punters feeling short-changed.

And let's not forget that, in 2020, boyband 'supergroup' Boyz on Block recorded a new version of 'Stay Another Day', although somehow – almost unbelievably – the combined talent of Abz Love from 5ive, Shane Lynch from Boyzone, Dane Bowers from Another Level, and Ben Ofoedu from dance duo Phats & Small failed to break into the top 100. (The same fate befell their follow-up – a cover of K-Ci & JoJo's 1998 number eight, 'All My Life').

NUMBER TWO
MARIAH CAREY
'ALL I WANT FOR CHRISTMAS IS YOU'

Stay with us to the end of this book to find out how the story ends for 'All I Want for Christmas Is You' (not to be confused with actress Dora Bryan's Christmas 1963 number-twenty hit, 'All I Want for Christmas Is a Beatle'). For now, suffice to say that, without this festive classic, Mariah's chart-topping success would only comprise covers of other people's hits. She first reached

1994
CHRISTMAS TOP TEN

1 East 17
'Stay Another Day'

2 Mariah Carey
'All I Want for Christmas Is You'

3 Oasis
'Whatever'

4 Boyzone
'Love Me for a Reason'

5 Rednex
'Cotton Eye Joe'

6 Celine Dion
'Think Twice'

7 Jimmy Nail
'Crocodile Shoes'

8 Zig and Zag
'Them Girls Them Girls'

9 Mighty Morphin Power Rangers
'Power Rangers'

10 Louis Armstrong
'We Have All the Time in the World'

number one in February 1994 with a cover of 'Without You', Nilsson's 1972 chart-topper, and then went back to number one for a second time in September 2000 when she teamed up with Westlife for a version of Phil Collins' 'Against All Odds' – a 1984 number two for Phil and later a 2005 chart-topper for one-hit wonder Steve Brookstein.

SOME OLDE CURIOSITIES

PART II

Meco feat. R2D2 and C3PO
'Sleigh Ride'
Released: 1980 (did not chart)
This single was taken from Domenico 'Meco' Monardo's *Star Wars* Christmas album, which included potential classics like 'What Can You Get a Wookiee for Christmas (When He Already Owns a Comb?)'.

Fogwell Flax and the Ankle Biters from Freehold Junior School
'One-Nine for Santa'
Chart peak: 68 (1981)
This was one of two 1981 spin-offs from TV programme *Tiswas*; the other was '(It's The) Year of the Pie' by the Pie 'N' Ears, whose line-up included Den Hegarty, a member of the 1977 Christmas top-ten band Darts.

Don Estelle with the Mold Green Junior Folk Group Choir
'Little Donkey'
Released: 1981 (did not chart)
This festive effort, issued on Don's very own Lofty record label, came from the smaller half of the duo (with Windsor Davies) who brought us the chart-topping 1975 single 'Whispering Grass'.

Dennis Waterman & George Cole
'What Are We Gonna Get 'Er Indoors?'
Chart peak: 21 (1983)
This hit was a spin-off from the ITV dramedy *Minder*, which ran for ten series between 1979 and 1989. The show's theme song, 'I Could Be So Good for You', was a number three for Dennis Waterman in November 1980.

Weather Girls
'Dear Santa (Bring Me a Man This Christmas)'
Released: 1983 (did not chart)
This was the follow-up to 'It's Raining Men', a hit that initially stalled at number seventy-three in 1983, but went on to peak at number two in March 1984 behind Lionel Richie's six-week chart-topper, 'Hello'.

The Krankies
'Hand in Hand at Christmas'
Released: 1984 (did not chart)
Although this single, from the album *The Krankies Go to Hollywood*, didn't make it into the Official Chart, Wee Jimmy Krankie appeared in the video for the 2007 Comic Relief chart-topper, '(I'm Gonna Be) 500 Miles', by the Proclaimers featuring Brian Potter and Andy Pipkin.

Keith Harris and Orville
'White Christmas'
Chart peak: 40 (1985)
This was the second top-forty single for ventriloquist Keith and his green sidekick, along with the 1982 number four 'Orville's Song'. Mantovani's 1952 instrumental version gave the conductor the first of his eight top-forty hits.

Frank Sidebottom
'Oh, Blimey, It's Christmas'
Chart peak: 87 (1985)
This single, the first of Frank's two attempts on the Christmas chart (the second was his 1986 *Christmas Is Really Fantastic* EP), included a unique take on Dream Academy's 1985 number fifteen, 'Life in a Northern Town'.

Spitting Image
'Santa Claus Is on The Dole'
Chart peak: 22 (1986)
This was the follow-up to 'The Chicken Song', which spent three weeks at number one in May 1986. Both singles had lyrics by Rob Grant and Doug Naylor, the creators of comedy sci-fi TV programme *Red Dwarf*.

Dame Edna Everage
'Spooky Christmas'
Chart peak: 83 (1988)
This cover was actually the B-side of Dame Edna's take on the theme song from TV soap *Neighbours*. By some spooky coincidence, the original version, by fellow Australian Barry Crocker, also peaked at number eighty-three.

Star Turn on 45 Pints
'Christmas Party'
Chart peak: 88 (1988)
The Turn reached number twelve earlier in 1988 with 'Pump Up the Bitter', their take on M|A|R|R|S's 1987 number one, 'Pump Up the Volume', though they have yet to return to the top forty.

Tony Robinson and the Angel Voices
'Christmas Wrapping'
Chart peak: 78 (1990)
This perfunctory attempt at the (not so) new rap thing from the *Blackadder* and *Time Team* mainstay was accompanied by the children of St Philip's Choir, Norbury.

Pinky and Perky
'Give Us a Kiss for Christmas'
Chart peak: 79 (1990)
This song was originally written by Lionel Bart – the man responsible for Tommy Steele's chart debut 'Rock With the Caveman' and Cliff Richard's first number one, 'Living Doll'. Puppet pigs Pinky and Perky also made number forty-seven in 1993 with their cover of Jackie Wilson's 'Reet Petite'.

Official Christmas Number 1

1995

MICHAEL JACKSON 'EARTH SONG'

WEEKS AT NUMBER ONE
6

FOLLOW-UP SINGLE: 'THEY DON'T CARE ABOUT US'
APRIL 1996

HIGHEST CHART POSITION
4

The sixth of Michael's seven chart-toppers, 'Earth Song' began its six-week reign – the singer's longest stay at number one – on 3 December, displacing a cover of Frankie Laine's 'I Believe' by actors Robson Green and Jerome Flynn. It was the third single from 1995's *HIStory* – Michael's only studio album to yield two chart-toppers (the first being 'You Are Not Alone') –

and marked a second number-one appearance for the Andraé Crouch Choir, who had supplied the rousing chorus on Madonna's 'Like a Prayer' in 1989.

Michael's performance of 'Earth Song' at the 1996 BRIT Awards (where he was collecting the never-to-be-repeated 'Artist of a Generation' award) prompted

27 March: *Forrest Gump* wins six Oscars at the sixty-seventh Academy Awards | **20 August:** After a

Pulp's Jarvis Cocker to express his derision by jumping on stage and pointing at his bottom – a stunt that led to Jarvis being questioned by police but not charged.

In his autobiography, Guy Pratt – bassist on 'Earth Song' – reported that Michael hid beneath a studio mixing desk during the recording and passed on instructions via an assistant, who would pretend that Michael was not in the room.

In 2018, the officialcharts.com website reported that 'Earth Song' was second only to 'Billie Jean' in popularity when sales of Michael's singles, downloads and audio streams were combined.

NUMBER TWO
MIKE FLOWERS POPS 'WONDERWALL'

While duplicate versions of the same song were commonplace in our early Christmas top tens, none occurred in the '70s and only one arose the following decade. (Refer back to Christmas 1987 for competing versions of 'When I Fall in Love' by both Rick Astley and Nat 'King' Cole.) 'Wonderwall' bucked that trend in December 1995.

The brainchild of Liverpudlian Mike Roberts, the Mike Flowers Pops rose to fame when *Radio 1*

1995
CHRISTMAS TOP TEN

1. **Michael Jackson**
   'Earth Song'

2. **Mike Flowers Pops**
   'Wonderwall'

3. **Boyzone**
   'Father and Son'

4. **Björk**
   'It's Oh So Quiet'

5. **Everything but the Girl**
   'Missing'

6. **Coolio feat. L.V.**
   'Gangsta's Paradise'

7. **Oasis**
   'Wonderwall'

8. **The Beatles**
   'Free as a Bird'

9. **Robson & Jerome**
   'I Believe'/'Up on the Roof'

10. **Eternal**
    'I Am Blessed'

Breakfast host Chris Evans told his listeners that the thirteen-piece band's Oasis cover was in fact the original version of 'Wonderwall'. Also known as MFP (their initials a knowing nod to budget record label Music for Pleasure), the band avoid entering our one-hit wonder category by dint of their 1996 covers of 'Light My Fire' and 'Don't Cry for Me Argentina', which charted at number thirty-nine and number thirty, respectively.

fierce chart battle, Blur's 'Country House' beats Oasis's 'Roll with It' to number one

1996

SPICE GIRLS '2 BECOME 1'

FOLLOW-UP SINGLE: 'MAMA'/'WHO DO YOU THINK YOU ARE'
MARCH 1997

WEEKS AT NUMBER ONE 3

HIGHEST CHART POSITION 1

With first-week sales of 462,000 copies, '2 Become 1' was the Spice Girls' third number one in six months and the second of eight singles to debut at the top. It would go on to be their second million-seller. When '2 Become 1' was revealed as Christmas number one on 22 December, the group's previous release, 'Say You'll Be There', was still in the top twenty, while their debut, 'Wannabe', was also hanging around at number fifty-nine. All three Spice Girls releases finished in the top ten for the year and 'Wannabe' was 1996's second best-selling single behind the Fugees' 'Killing Me Softly'.

'2 Become 1' was the only Spice Girls Christmas chart-topper (spoiler alert: they get two more) to appear on the 2020 top-twenty list of all-time best-selling Christmas number ones, though it also suffered the biggest drop of their eight number ones, falling to number six in mid-January.

To boost their Christmas credentials, a 'giftpack' edition of the CD single included a cover of Leroy Anderson's festive favourite 'Sleigh Ride' (also a number-six hit for S Club Juniors in 2002) and a 'signed' picture postcard, though it seems only Mel B got the 'smile for the camera' memo.

1 March: Status Quo take BBC Radio 1 to court, claiming the station refuses to play their latest single |

'2 Become 1' was released in the US the following July and peaked at number four. However, with one eye (or perhaps five) on the Hispanic market, the girls also recorded a Spanish version of the song, 'Seremos Uno Los Dos', with new lyrics by Nacho Mañó.

More than two decades later, Emma 'Baby Spice' Bunton recorded the song as a duet with Robbie Williams for her 2019 solo album, *My Happy Place*.

NUMBER TWO
DUNBLANE
'KNOCKIN' ON HEAVEN'S DOOR'/'THROW THESE GUNS AWAY'

Following the tragic mass shooting at Dunblane Primary School on 13 March 1996, Bob Dylan gave musician Ted Christopher permission to adapt his 1973 single 'Knockin' on Heaven's Door' for release as a charity fundraiser. The sales proceeds were shared between Save the Children, Childline and the Children's Hospice Association of Scotland.

The new recording, featuring a children's choir and a guitar solo by Dire Straits' Mark Knopfler, was recorded at Abbey Road Studios and released on 9 December. It

1996
CHRISTMAS TOP TEN

1. **Spice Girls**
   '2 Become 1'
2. **Dunblane**
   'Knockin' on Heaven's Door'/
   'Throw These Guns Away'
3. **Madonna**
   'Don't Cry for Me Argentina'
4. **Toni Braxton**
   'Un-Break My Heart'
5. **Robert Miles feat. Maria Nayler**
   'One & One'
6. **Boyzone**
   'A Different Beat'
7. **The Prodigy**
   'Breathe'
8. **Mark Morrison**
   'Horny'
9. **Celine Dion**
   'All by Myself'
10. **Beautiful South**
    'Don't Marry Her'

became the twenty-sixth number one of 1996, with the Spice Girls delaying the release of their single by a week out of respect.

A 1992 cover of 'Knockin' on Heaven's Door' by American rockers Guns N' Roses proved to be the biggest of the band's seventeen top-forty hits, charting at number two behind 'Please Don't Go' by KWS.

1997

SPICE GIRLS 'TOO MUCH'

FOLLOW-UP SINGLE: 'STOP'
MARCH 1998

WEEKS AT NUMBER ONE
2

HIGHEST CHART POSITION
2

'Too Much' was written in breaks from filming *Spice World*, but clearly fans detected no let-up in quality as the single became the group's sixth consecutive number one in less than eighteen months. It also saw the Spice Girls become the first act to top the Official Chart with their first six singles and the first act to have five consecutive singles enter the Official Chart at number one. In the US, 'Too Much' reached number nine – an improvement on their previous release, 'Spice Up Your Life', which stalled at number eighteen – but it was their fourth and final single to break the American top ten.

'Too Much' spent two weeks at number one – having fought off bookmakers' favourite, the theme tune from BBC children's TV programme *Teletubbies* – only to be replaced by another BBC project in the form of 'Perfect Day', a charity single released as part of the *Children in Need* campaign.

30 March: Channel 5 launches in the UK | 3 May: UK act Katrina and the Waves win the Eurovision

A promo video for 'Too Much' – directed by Howard Greenhalgh, a frequent collaborator with Pet Shop Boys – premiered on the US UPN TV channel as part of a one-hour special titled *Too Much Is Never Enough*. On the programme, each of the five Spice Girls – or, as one press release described them, the 'spicy quintet' – was interviewed by R&B singer Brandy. The aforementioned press release also mentioned the girls' usual nicknames ('Baby', 'Posh', 'Scary' and 'Sporty'), with the exception of Geri 'Ginger' Halliwell, who was instead dubbed 'Sexy Spice'. Other promotional activity included hosting *An Audience with...* – the first pop group to do so – in front of an all-female audience and entertaining Her Majesty the Queen at the *Royal Variety Performance*.

NUMBER TWO
TELETUBBIES
'TELETUBBIES SAY "EH-OH!"'

As Tinky Winky, Dipsy, Laa-Laa and Po failed to release a second single from their album (even though 'Puddle Dance', 'Dirty Knees' and 'Dipsy's Fancy Hat' were all rumoured to be the follow-up), we must add the Teletubbies to our list of one-hit wonders. However, sales of more than a million copies also earn them a place on the list of all-time best-selling debut releases.

1997
CHRISTMAS TOP TEN

1 **Spice Girls**
'Too Much'

2 **Teletubbies**
'Teletubbies say "Eh-Oh!"'

3 **Various Artists**
'Perfect Day'

4 **All Saints**
'Never Ever'

5 **Janet Jackson**
'Together Again'

6 **Aqua**
'Barbie Girl'

7 **Robbie Williams**
'Angels'

8 **Natalie Imbruglia**
'Torn'

9 **Boyzone**
'Baby Can I Hold You'/
'Shooting Star'

10 **Ma$e**
'Feel So Good'

Topping the Official Chart the week before Christmas, the single didn't include performer credits, but it did start with laughter from the 'Sun Baby', played in the television series by Jessica Smith, aged approximately seven months, so there is a strong chance that Jessica is the youngest person to ever appear on a number one.

Official Christmas Number 1

1998

SPICE GIRLS 'GOODBYE'

WEEKS AT NUMBER ONE 1

FOLLOW-UP SINGLE: 'HOLLER'/ 'LET LOVE LEAD THE WAY' NOVEMBER 2000

HIGHEST CHART POSITION 1

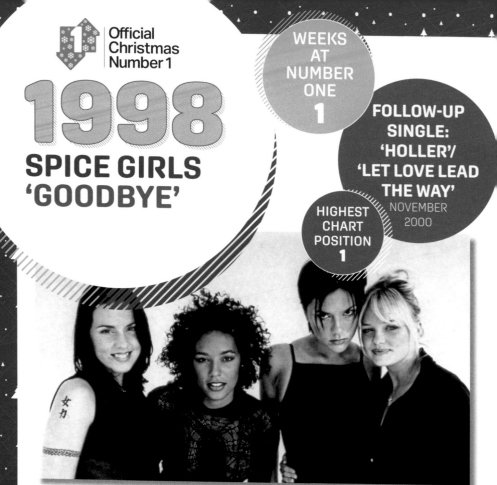

On 31 May 1998, the BBC News website broke the story that Geri Halliwell had left the Spice Girls under the headline 'Ginger Snaps'. A week later, *Top of the Pops* showed a pre-recorded performance of the quintet singing 'Viva Forever' and then the four remaining girls set off to fulfil the American leg of their Spiceworld tour. Songwriting partners Richard 'Biff' Stannard and Matt Rowe flew to the States to work with the group on new material and, lo, the Spice Girls claimed an eighth number-one single and became the second act (after the Beatles) to have three consecutive Christmas chart-toppers. 'Goodbye' entered the chart on 20 December, knocking aside B*Witched, pretenders to the Spice throne, who had just had their third number one with 'To You I Belong'.

9 May: Israel's Dana International wins the Eurovision Song Contest with 'Diva' | 29 August: Anthony

In its first week on sale, 'Goodbye' sold over 380,000 copies, finishing eighth in the best-selling singles of 1998. The girls upped the festive ante again by including a cover of the Waitresses' 'Christmas Wrapping' on the CD single. Lucky fans in the US were also treated to live versions of 'Sisters Are Doin' It for Themselves' and 'We Are Family'.

In addition to the group's chart-topper, a glance at this year's Christmas top ten shows Melanie C notching up her first solo hit, though it was Melanie B who stole a march on all the other girls – solo Geri included – when 'I Want You Back' went to number one in September. The single was a collaboration between Mel B and Missy 'Misdemeanor' Elliott that saw the latter become the first female rapper to top the UK Official Chart.

NUMBER TWO
CHEF
'CHOCOLATE SALTY BALLS (P.S. I LOVE YOU)'

Despite their previous good form in the number-one stakes, the Spice Girls had to fight off strong opposition from Chef (voiced by soul legend Isaac Hayes), a character from the cartoon *South Park*. When the shops closed on Saturday 19 December after the busiest week of the year, 'Goodbye'

1998
CHRISTMAS TOP TEN

1 Spice Girls
'Goodbye'

2 Chef
'Chocolate Salty Balls (P.S. I Love You)'

3 Denise and Johnny
'Especially for You'

4 Cher
'Believe'

5 B*Witched
'To You I Belong'

6 Steps
'Heartbeat'/'Tragedy'

7 Honeyz
'End of the Line'

8 Bryan Adams feat. Melanie C.
'When You're Gone'

9 Billie
'She Wants You'

10 Jane McDonald
'Cruise into Christmas'

bested 'Chocolate Salty Balls' by fewer than 8,000 sales (2 per cent of the girls' total), but Isaac had his revenge the following week when he ousted the group by a similarly slim margin.

South Park would gift us another Christmas top-ten hit a year later when 'Mr Hankey, the Christmas Poo' reached number eight.

'Ant' McPartlin, Declan 'Dec' Donnelly and Cat Deeley present the first episode of *CD:UK* on ITV

1999

WESTLIFE
'I HAVE A DREAM'/
'SEASONS IN THE SUN'

FOLLOW-UP SINGLE: 'FOOL AGAIN'
APRIL 2000

WEEKS AT NUMBER ONE
4

HIGHEST CHART POSITION
1

The Christmas release was one of Westlife's fourteen chart-toppers (starting with 'Swear It Again' in May 1999 and ending with 'The Rose' in November 2006) to enter the Official Chart straight at number one. It was also the boys' fourth number-one single of the year and – by virtue of staying at the top until the middle of the following January – the very first number one of the twenty-first century.

Westlife cornered the Christmas market with two cover versions on one double A-side single. The first track was a cover of 'I Have a Dream' – ABBA's own attempt at Christmas number one back in 1979 when they were pipped to the top by Pink Floyd's 'Another Brick in the Wall (Part II)' – and the second was a version of Terry Jacks' cheerful tale of a dying man's last words, 'Seasons in the Sun', which originally spent

11 January: TV sitcom *The League of Gentlemen* begins on BBC Two | **1 June:** Music-focused

three weeks at number one in 1974. Westlife's winning combination would ultimately become their second best-selling single, bettered only by their 2001 cover of Billy Joel's 'Uptown Girl'.

This was a good year for Irish acts generally, with four of them spending a combined total of ten weeks at number one. For 'acts' read 'extended family', as Westlife (five weeks) were managed by Ronan Keating (one week solo), who was a member of Boyzone (three weeks) alongside Shane Lynch, the brother of twins Edele and Keavy of B*Witched (one week).

NUMBER TWO
CLIFF RICHARD
'THE MILLENNIUM PRAYER'

After three weeks at the summit, Cliff's fourteenth and most recent number one looked all set to become his fourth Christmas chart-topper – until Westlife stole his thunder at the very last minute.

Between 'Move It', his very first Official Chart entry in 1958, and '21st Century Christmas' in 2006, Cliff has had eleven unique hits stall at number two, racking up a combined total of twenty-three weeks in second place. Madonna has been a runner-up twelve times – if we count the two number-two

1. **Westlife**
   'I Have a Dream'/'Seasons in the Sun'

2. **Cliff Richard**
   'The Millennium Prayer'

3. **John Lennon**
   'Imagine'

4. **Cuban Boys**
   'Cognoscenti vs Intelligentsia'

5. **S Club 7**
   'Two in a Million'/'You're My Number One'

6. **Artful Dodger feat. Craig David**
   'Re-Rewind (The Crowd Say Bo Selecta)'

7. **Steps**
   'Say You'll Be Mine'/'Better the Devil You Know'

8. **Mr Hankey**
   'Mr Hankey, the Christmas Poo'

9. **William Orbit**
   'Barber's Adagio for Strings'

10. **Vengaboys**
    'Kiss (When the Sun Don't Shine)'

spells for 'Crazy for You' separately – but only for a total of thirteen weeks, while Kylie Minogue has also stalled in second place on eleven occasions, but is still three weeks shy of Cliff's total stay.

NOTES FROM THE HIT FACTORY

Pete Waterman's part in the Christmas number one...

Dr Pete Waterman OBE is an author, DJ, TV presenter and railway expert, though he is perhaps best known as one-third of the hugely successful music production and song-writing team Stock Aitken Waterman, as well as for his world-famous PWL (now PWE) label.

His influence on the Christmas top ten was first felt in 1977 when, as a young promotions executive, he helped Ruby Winters to number four with her Official Chart debut, 'I Will' (one place above the first UK entry for Bing Crosby's

'White Christmas'). Since then, Pete has been involved in more than twenty number-one hits with artists including Dead or Alive, Kylie Minogue, Rick Astley, Bananarama, Steps, Mel and Kim, Cliff Richard, and Jason Donovan. However, most importantly for our story is his involvement in the Christmas number-one singles by Band Aid II and Westlife. Over to you, Pete:

Band Aid II came as a bit of a shock. To say we were busy in 1989 is an understatement; Matt [Aitken], Mike [Stock] and I had agreed between us that we would stop work at the end of November and not come back until January. We had an amazing Christmas party planned at the Savoy Hotel and, as I was getting dressed, the phone went and the receptionist said, 'Pete, I've got Bob Geldof for you.' Bob said, 'Pete, it's your turn now. We need another Band Aid, so it's over to you. I'm stepping out, you can step in.'

I told the studio staff that they could have the next day off, but I needed them all back for work on Saturday at eight o'clock. There's a picture of the three of us on the Sunday night that looks faked – but it wasn't. We were completely and utterly knackered. Great fun but really hard work.

The first people I called were the four artists who could have had the Christmas number one because it was most likely going to be Kylie, Jason, Bros or Cliff Richard. It showed that these people understood what Band Aid meant and would even stop themselves getting to number one to support this project. They were literally putting their hands in their own pockets. I'm not sure I was popular with all their record companies, but the artists understood.

The previous year, we'd had three in the Christmas top ten: Kylie and Jason's 'Especially for You' at number two; Angry Anderson at number four; and a remix of the Four Tops' 'Loco in Acapulco' at number nine. Angry Anderson was one we didn't originally want to do; I didn't even want it on our label. Imagine if Kylie and Jason had been kept off number one by Angry Anderson – Matt and Mike would have killed me!

In 1998, we got 'Especially for You' back into the Christmas top ten with Denise van Outen and Johnny Vaughan. We thought it was funny, but they took it very seriously. Denise loved the record – she knew it inside out and backwards and wanted to sound just like Kylie. That's another record we hadn't planned to do, but the public and Woolworths – the biggest seller of singles then – talked us into it.

The ironic thing for me personally is that we never did a Christmas album. In hindsight, that was incredibly naive of us. Our weakness was that we would sometimes look at the commercial thing to do and think it was too obvious.

Westlife is one of those hit records that people forget is a Stock Aitken Waterman production. We had an approach to make an ABBA charity album, so I enrolled Steps straight away and went to Simon Cowell to see if Westlife would participate. He said, 'Yes, if they can do "I Have a Dream".' The problem was Cliff Richard! We knew he was our biggest threat and was almost guaranteed the top spot with 'The Millennium Prayer'.

I was in India, fishing in the middle of the jungle, when I saw a two-day-old copy

of *The Times* saying that Cliff would be number one. Mobile phone signals were difficult to get, but I found some high ground, got through to Simon and said, 'I see we've lost.' He said, 'Trust me.' Cliff had been ahead on the midweek reports, but we overtook him in the last few days and – *bang* – Christmas number one!

Then, in 2002, when Girls Aloud topped the Official Chart ahead of One True Voice and the Cheeky Girls, I effectively had numbers one, two and three in the Christmas top ten because *Popstars: The Rivals* was my TV show!

Christmas number ones have always been important to me. Ever since I was a kid, they really fascinated me. It was the time of year when I paid more attention to radio because I was off school and my mum was an avid radio listener. Songs like Dickie Valentine's 'Christmas Alphabet' have really stuck in my mind. I loved Winifred Atwell's Christmas number one, 'Let's Have Another Party'.

That said, my favourite Christmas number one is Johnny Mathis, 'When a Child Is Born' – one of the greatest pop records ever made. He's probably not in my all-time top ten like the Beatles or Bowie or Marvin Gaye, but I did idolise Johnny. He was the only artist who I wanted to produce but never got to: we did the deal with Johnny and his manager, but we couldn't get his record label to agree.

The Christmas number one used to be all about radio, then it was television, then social media – but something will come along and change that. It wouldn't worry me if they amended the rules and one of my old tracks never got in the Official Chart again; I'm a big advocate of letting new talent have its chance.

WELCOME TO THE '00s

The first decade of the new millennium was all about the screen. Though the influence of cinema's 'silver' screen slowed, our TV screen began to make or break acts literally overnight – and aiding the role of both these screens were the screens of computers, mobile phones and iPods.

While not quite as significant as in the previous decade, having a hit film to help spread awareness of a song was still a nice bonus. Cinematic releases in the '00s helped to drive chart-topping singles for a number of artists, including: All Saints ('Pure Shores', *The Beach*); Destiny's Child ('Independent Women Part I', *Charlie's Angels*); Geri Halliwell ('It's Raining Men', *Bridget Jones's Diary*); Christina Aguilera, Lil' Kim, Mýa and Pink ('Lady Marmalade', *Moulin Rouge!*); and Michael Andrews featuring Gary Jules ('Mad World', *Donnie Darko*).

It was also a time when the jukebox musical became a good way to repackage old songs. Although building a stage show around an existing repertoire wasn't a completely new concept (we might think of *Mamma Mia!* as having kickstarted this bigger trend, but an earlier ABBA musical, *Abbacadabra*, actually debuted in London back in 1983), the format grew in popularity in the '00s. This resulted in musicals – with plots of varying flimsiness

– built around the songbooks of artists including Queen, Madness, Rod Stewart, Frankie Valli and the Four Seasons, Boney M., Take That, and the Proclaimers.

One of the most significant developments of the decade began in January 2001 when ITV introduced the reality talent show *Popstars*. After hanging in there for thirteen weeks, the viewing public had no hesitation in sending winners Hear'Say to number one with their debut single, 'Pure and Simple'. Liberty X, comprising the show's runners-up, also topped the Official Chart with 'Just a Little'. The two acts would go on to have fourteen top-forty hits between them.

Later the same year came *Pop Idol*, which gave us Will Young and his million-selling number-one debut, 'Anything Is Possible'/'Evergreen', as well as Gareth Gates, the fourth artist to take a version of 'Unchained Melody' to number one. Both would confound their critics, racking up a further twenty-two top-forty hits between them, including three number ones each and a chart-topping duet version of the Beatles' 'The Long and Winding Road'. But it didn't stop there. This veritable hit factory of a first series also produced Darius and the chart-topping 'Colourblind', plus individual top-forty hits for Zoe Birkett, Rosie Ribbons, Jessica Garlick and Rik Waller.

In 2002, ITV launched *Popstars: The Rivals*, resulting in that year's Christmas number one, number two and number three, courtesy of, respectively, Girls Aloud, One True Voice and the Cheeky Girls. Yet these shows were just warming the TV audience up for *The X Factor*. All of its winners in the '00s would have number-one singles – four of those in Christmas week – and their stories unfold in the coming pages. By 2009, the series finale attracted 19 million viewers, making *The X Factor* the most popular programme on UK TV.

Britain's Got Talent arrived on our screens in 2007, launching the career of operatic tenor Paul Potts. Of all the show's alumni, Susan Boyle was undoubtedly the most successful, with her version of 'I Dreamed a Dream', from the musical *Les Misérables*, becoming a transatlantic hit after it was seen over 250 million times on YouTube – another indication of the influence of new technology.

TV also gave a boost to performers who had been away from the limelight. After winning the 2004 series of *I'm a Celebrity ... Get Me Out of Here!*, Peter Andre re-issued his 1996 single 'Mysterious Girl' and went to number one after a six-year Official Chart absence. There was also a welcome return for our old Christmas number-one friend Shakin' Stevens, who had his first top-forty hit in thirteen years with a cover of Pink's 'Trouble', following a stint on the 2005 ITV series *Hit Me, Baby, One More Time*.

One victim of the changing times was *Top of the Pops*. In 2005, the show was moved to a Sunday evening slot on BBC Two, reportedly so it could broadcast immediately after the new top-forty countdown on Radio 1. However, viewing figures continued to dwindle and, finally, in July 2006, after more than forty years and 2,200 episodes, the studio lights were turned out for the last time. The final 'it's number one, it's *Top of the Pops*' single was 'Hips Don't Lie' by Shakira featuring Wyclef Jean.

The dramatic change in what we watched coincided with an equally seismic shift in how we bought our music. In 2001, Apple launched the iPod, and access to legal downloads via the UK iTunes Store followed in 2004. By the middle of the decade, more people were choosing to buy downloads than CD singles, with the former counting towards the Official Singles Chart as of 2005. In March 2006, 'Pump It' by the Black Eyed Peas became the first top-forty hit from downloads alone. A month later, Gnarls Barkley's debut single, 'Crazy', went all the way to number one without the need for a single buyer to enter a record store.

Instant access to millions of tracks began to have a significant and sometimes unexpected impact on the Official Chart. Look no further than Mint Royale's 2005 number-twenty hit, 'Singin' in the Rain', which, after soundtracking the dance routine of *Britain's Got Talent* contestant George Sampson, went from selling fewer than fifty copies a week to spending two weeks at number one in June 2008. The year before, a campaign led by broadcaster Danny Baker resulted in 'The Ladies' Bras' – a wonderfully irreverent song by Jonny Trunk and Wisbey – peaking at number twenty-seven and becoming the shortest Official Chart hit ever. (At thirty-six seconds long, it broke the one-minute-and-four-seconds record set only two months earlier by Hans Zimmer's 'Spider Pig', which featured in the *The Simpsons Movie*.)

At the end of 2009, the chart-toppers seeing out the decade included *X Factor* winner Alexandra Burke, runners-up JLS, and a cover of 'You Are Not Alone' by that year's finalists. The show's judges got in on the act, too, as Cheryl Cole's solo debut, 'Fight for This Love', went to number one and Simon Cowell's Syco record label closed the decade with twenty-three chart-toppers – more than any of its competitors. Surely the programme-makers, label bosses and technology titans would now dictate what went on in the charts and who the Christmas number ones would be?

Let's find out...

2000

BOB THE BUILDER
'CAN WE FIX IT?'

FOLLOW-UP SINGLE: 'MAMBO NO. 5'
SEPTEMBER 2001

WEEKS AT NUMBER ONE
3

HIGHEST CHART POSITION
1

At the end of a year that produced a record forty-two different chart-toppers, Westlife had to hand their Christmas number-one crown to Bob, voiced by actor Neil Morrissey. The biggest-selling single by a non-human solo artist (admittedly a niche category), 'Can We Fix It?' was taken from Bob's number-four debut collection, *Bob the Builder: The Album*. This album also featured a duet version of 'Crocodile Rock' with Elton John, as well as Bob's follow-up single, 'Mambo No. 5' – the latter making him the first 'novelty' act to top the Official Chart twice.

In addition to topping the Australian chart, 'Can We Fix It?' had a couple of international releases, too – in Finland as 'Puuha-Pete Kaiken Korjaa' by Puuha-Pete, and in the Benelux countries as 'Kunnen Wij Het Maken?' by Bob de Bouwer.

5 March: Singer Gary Barlow makes his acting debut in the 150th episode of police drama *Heartbeat* |

'Can We Fix It?' finished the year as the best-selling single of 2000, ahead of All Saints' 'Pure Shores', and it has now sold more than a million copies. Music to the ears, no doubt, of its songwriter, Paul K. Joyce, previously part of '80s synth-pop trio Sense, whose debut single, 'Three Minutes Later', was produced by Dave Ball – a 1981 chart-topper with Soft Cell.

In April 2001, 'Can We Fix It?' appeared on *NOW That's What I Call Music!: Volume 48* betwixt Kylie Minogue and Eva Cassidy, though 'difficult second album syndrome' resulted in a seven-year wait for Bob's sophomore collection, *Never Mind the Breeze Blocks*. Unfortunately, his audience had moved on (or possibly grown up) by this time, so his third single, 'Big Fish Little Fish', stalled at a disappointing number eighty-one.

NUMBER TWO
WESTLIFE
'WHAT MAKES A MAN'

After seven consecutive number-one hits, Westlife ceded to the better (animated) man when Bob the Builder thwarted their bid for a second Christmas chart-topper. And waiting for Christmas gift purchases to go away didn't work either; when Bob was knocked from the top on 7 January, it

2000
CHRISTMAS TOP TEN

1 Bob the Builder
'Can We Fix It?'

2 Westlife
'What Makes a Man'

3 Eminem
'Stan'

4 S Club 7
'Never Had a Dream Come True'

5 Baha Men
'Who Let the Dogs Out'

6 Oxide & Neutrino feat. Megaman, Romeo and Lisa Maffia
'No Good 4 Me'

7 LeAnn Rimes
'Can't Fight the Moonlight'

8 Tweenies
'No. 1'

9 Destiny's Child
'Independent Women Part I'

10 Robbie Williams
'Supreme'

was one-hit wonder Rui Da Silva featuring Cassandra with 'Touch Me' that took over, making DJ Rui the first Portuguese artist to top the Official Charts. The New Year wasn't all bad for Westlife, though, with the Comic Relief charity single 'Uptown Girl' going straight to number one in March, followed by the group's ninth chart-topper, 'Queen of My Heart', in November.

18 December: Singer and songwriter Kirsty MacColl dies, aged forty-one

Official Christmas Number 1

WEEKS AT NUMBER ONE
3

2001

ROBBIE WILLIAMS AND NICOLE KIDMAN 'SOMETHIN' STUPID'

ROBBIE WILLIAMS' FOLLOW-UP SINGLE: 'FEEL' DECEMBER 2002

HIGHEST CHART POSITION 4

NICOLE KIDMAN'S FOLLOW-UP SINGLE: 'ONE DAY I'LL FLY AWAY' DECEMBER 2002

HIGHEST CHART POSITION 79

This duet was the fifth of seven number-one singles for Robbie as a solo artist, though he also topped the Official Chart seven times with Take That and four times on charity singles, including the 2012 Christmas number one. By contrast, this is Nicole's sole number one, though it did make her the twelfth Australian artist to top the Official Chart and the third winner of an Academy Award for Best Actress to do so (after Barbra Streisand and Cher, if you were wondering).

'Somethin' Stupid' was written by C. Carson Parks and first recorded by him and his wife Gaile in 1966. The following year, Frank Sinatra and his daughter Nancy took their version to number one, while a 1995 cover by UB40's Ali Campbell and

his daughter Kibibi reached number thirty. (The next father–daughter combination to top the Official Chart was Ozzy and Kelly Osbourne with 'Changes' in 2003.)

For Nicole, 'Somethin' Stupid' was the second of three hits. It was released in between 'Come What May' – a duet with Ewan McGregor that had reached number twenty-seven two months earlier – and a 2002 cover of 'One Day I'll Fly Away', originally a number two for Randy Crawford in 1980. Both singles were taken from the soundtrack of *Moulin Rouge!*, directed by Nicole's Australian compatriot Baz Luhrmann – himself a chart-topping one-hit wonder, courtesy of his 1999 number one, 'Everybody's Free (To Wear Sunscreen)'.

NUMBER TWO
GORDON HASKELL
'HOW WONDERFUL YOU ARE'

And from one one-hit wonder to another. Dorset-born singer and songwriter Gordon Haskell began his varied career in the Fleur de Lys, a mid-'60s psychedelic band, before a brief spell with prog rockers King Crimson, sharing vocal duties with our 1975 Christmas number-two artist, Greg Lake.

After a few decades touring pubs and small clubs as a solo artist,

2001
CHRISTMAS TOP TEN

1 **Robbie Williams and Nicole Kidman**
'Somethin' Stupid'

2 **Gordon Haskell**
'How Wonderful You Are'

3 **Daniel Bedingfield**
'Gotta Get Thru This'

4 **Sophie Ellis-Bextor**
'Murder on the Dancefloor'

5 **Stereophonics**
'Handbags and Gladrags'

6 **S Club 7**
'Have You Ever'

7 **Ian Van Dahl**
'Will I?'

8 **Samantha Mumba**
'Lately'

9 **Tweenies**
'I Believe in Christmas'

10 **Hermes House Band**
'Country Roads'

55-year-old Gordon was propelled straight to number two when 'How Wonderful You Are' was picked up by Radio 2, despite the ballad having only been released by a small independent record label. A similarly pleasant fate befell Gordon's 2002 album, *Harry's Bar*, which would have topped the chart had it not been for those Welsh rockers Stereophonics.

Beatle George Harrison dies, aged fifty-eight | 18 December: Singer and songwriter Billie Eilish born

Official Christmas Number 1

2002

GIRLS ALOUD 'SOUND OF THE UNDERGROUND'

WEEKS AT NUMBER ONE
4

FOLLOW-UP SINGLE: 'NO GOOD ADVICE'
MAY 2003

HIGHEST CHART POSITION
2

After the 2001 TV talent show *Popstars* gave the world Hear'Say (four top-forty hits, two number ones) and Liberty X (eight top-forty hits, one number one), 2002 brought us *Popstars: The Rivals*, pitching Girls Aloud against One True Voice in a battle for the Christmas number-one spot. The girls were armed with pop banger 'Sound of the Underground', while the boys went with a two-pronged attack, combining a cover of the Bee Gees' 'Sacred Trust' with a Pete Waterman-penned original, 'After You're Gone'. The girls' first-week sales were almost 50 per cent greater, propelling them to the top of the Official Chart with what would be the first of their whopping twenty-two top-forty hits and four number ones.

11 March: Digital radio station BBC 6 Music launches | 26 May: Reality TV series *The Osbournes* makes

Girls Aloud's not-so-secret weapon was the songwriting and production team Xenomania, responsible for more than forty top-forty hits, including the chart-topping 'Believe' by Cher and 'Hole in the Head' by Sugababes – a fellow girl group who would go on to collaborate with Girls Aloud in 2007. The combined talent of the two acts was unleashed on a chart-topping cover of the 1986 Run-DMC/Aerosmith hit, 'Walk This Way', released in aid of Comic Relief.

After Girls Aloud split in 2013, Cheryl (occasionally Cheryl Cole) became the first British female solo artist to have five number-one singles – a record surpassed by Jess Glynne in 2018.

NUMBER TWO
ONE TRUE VOICE
'SACRED TRUST'/'AFTER YOU'RE GONE (I'LL STILL BE LOVING YOU)'

Having come so close with their debut single, One True Voice gave it another go with 'Shakespeare's (Way With) Words'. The curious (way with) brackets and a co-writing credit for Rick Astley helped the single reach number ten in June 2003, though this wasn't enough to keep the quintet together after a planned tour was cancelled due to poor ticket sales.

2002
CHRISTMAS TOP TEN

1 Girls Aloud
'Sound of the Underground'

2 One True Voice
'Sacred Trust'/'After You're Gone (I'll Still Be Loving You)'

3 Cheeky Girls
'Cheeky Song (Touch My Bum)'

4 Blue feat. Elton John
'Sorry Seems to Be the Hardest Word'

5 Eminem
'Lose Yourself'

6 Daniel Bedingfield
'If You're Not the One'

7 Love Inc.
'You're a Superstar'

8 Las Ketchup
'The Ketchup Song (Aserejé)'

9 Avril Lavigne
'Sk8er Boi'

10 Robbie Williams
'Feel'

There was also a place in the 2002 Christmas top ten for failed *Popstars: The Rivals* auditionees the Cheeky Girls. 'Cheeky Song (Touch My Bum)' was one of five top-forty hits for the twins, including a second attempt on the festive chart with 'Have a Cheeky Christmas', which reached number ten in December 2003.

Official Christmas Number 1

2003

MICHAEL ANDREWS FEAT. GARY JULES 'MAD WORLD'

WEEKS AT NUMBER ONE 3

GARY JULES' FOLLOW-UP SINGLE: 'BROKE WINDOW' APRIL 2004

HIGHEST CHART POSITION 83

Perhaps the British public were growing tired of boy bands and girl groups when they decided that what they really, really wanted for Christmas was a funereal ballad about 'dreams in which I'm dying' taken from a cult film centred around death with a bit of paranoia thrown in for good measure.

American musicians Michael Andrews and Gary Jules recorded their version of Tears for Fears' 1982 number-three hit for the 2001

12 January: Maurice Gibb of the Bee Gees dies, aged fifty-three | 4 November: Channel 4 soap *Brookside*

psychological thriller *Donnie Darko*. When the film was released on DVD, demand for the soundtrack prompted the release of 'Mad World' as an unlikely Christmas single. The film included a role for Patrick Swayze, who had his own top-forty hit in 1988 with 'She's Like the Wind' – a number-seventeen collaboration with Wendy Fraser, taken from the *Dirty Dancing* soundtrack.

After three weeks, 'Mad World' was replaced at the top by 'All This Time' – the debut single from Michelle McManus, winner of reality TV show *Pop Idol*. Michelle also graces our Christmas top ten on the Idols' cover of John and Yoko's 'Happy Xmas (War Is Over)'.

NUMBER TWO
THE DARKNESS
'CHRISTMAS TIME (DON'T LET THE BELLS END)'

Tongue-in-cheek rockers the Darkness had already reached number two back in September with 'I Believe in a Thing Called Love', though they were kept from the top by 'Where Is the Love?' – the first of five Black Eyed Peas number ones. For their attempt on the Christmas chart, the Darkness enlisted the services of producer Bob Ezrin – the man behind the mixing desk on our 1979 Christmas number one, Pink Floyd's 'Another Brick in

2003
CHRISTMAS TOP TEN

1 Michael Andrews feat. Gary Jules
'Mad World'

2 The Darkness
'Christmas Time (Don't Let the Bells End)'

3 Ozzy & Kelly Osbourne
'Changes'

4 *Bo' Selecta!*
'Proper Crimbo'

5 The Idols
'Happy Xmas (War Is Over)'

6 Will Young
'Leave Right Now'

7 Black Eyed Peas
'Shut Up'

8 Atomic Kitten
'Ladies Night'

9 Shane Richie
'I'm Your Man'

10 Sugababes
'Too Lost in You'

the Wall (Part II)' – along with the Haberdashers' Aske's Hatcham College Choir, who featured on East 17's 1997 number three, 'Hey Child'.

A week before Christmas, the BBC News website reported that the Darkness were bookies' favourite for the top slot, but, once again, the British record-buying public proved unpredictable.

2004

BAND AID 20
'DO THEY KNOW
IT'S CHRISTMAS?'

**WEEKS
AT
NUMBER
ONE
4**

In a bid to raise funds for famine relief in the troubled Darfur region of western Sudan, the Band Aid machine sparked into life once more, with production duties falling to Nigel Godrich, who was able to call upon recent employers Paul McCartney, Radiohead, Travis, and the Divine Comedy.

Notably, the larger cast featured more female performers than the two previous versions combined. Step forward Dido, Natasha Bedingfield, Ms Dynamite, Skye Edwards of Morcheeba, Estelle, Jamelia, Beverley Knight,

Shaznay Lewis of All Saints, Katie Melua, Róisín Murphy of Moloko, Rachel Stevens, Joss Stone, and Sugababes Keisha, Mutya and Heidi. At least four of these artists weren't born when the 1984 version of the song was recorded. Bono returned from that original line-up, though none of the 1989 artists were retained. The backing band featured Thom Yorke and Jonny Greenwood of Radiohead on piano and guitar, Justin and Dan Hawkins of the

---

29 February: *The Lord of the Rings: Return of the King* wins eleven Oscars at the seventy-sixth

Darkness on guitar, Paul McCartney on bass and Supergrass's Danny Goffey on drums. Blur's Damon Albarn turned up on the day to serve tea.

Released on 29 November, the single sold 72,000 copies in its first twenty-four hours and 200,000 CDs in its first week, becoming the biggest seller of 2004. Although downloads weren't chart-eligible at the time, the single was also available online, with digital platforms donating profits to the Band Aid Trust. Additionally, prompted by the DVD release of Live Aid, the CD single included a recording of 'Do They Know It's Christmas?' from the concert's 1985 finale at Wembley Stadium.

NUMBER TWO
RONAN KEATING
FEAT. YUSUF
'FATHER AND SON'

Singer and songwriter Cat Stevens originally recorded 'Father and Son' for his 1970 album *Tea for the Tillerman* and it was included on the flip of his 1971 single 'Moonshadow'.

In December 2004, Cat, who changed his name to Yusuf upon his conversion to Islam in 1977, released this duet version with Ronan. The former boy-bander made the laudable decision to

donate his royalties to Band Aid, as well as the more questionable decision to include a bangin' dance remix as a CD bonus track.

A look back at our 1995 Christmas top ten shows that Ronan had already covered 'Father and Son' with Boyzone, though that version narrowly missed out on the Christmas number-two spot.

2004
CHRISTMAS TOP TEN

1. **Band Aid 20**
'Do They Know It's Christmas?'

2. **Ronan Keating feat. Yusuf**
'Father and Son'

3. **Kylie Minogue**
'I Believe in You'

4. **Ice Cube feat. Mack 10 & Ms Toi**
'You Can Do It'

5. **Merrion, McCall & Kensit/
Bo' Selecta!**
'I Got You Babe'/'Soda Pop'

6. **Destiny's Child**
'Lose My Breath'

7. **Lemar**
'If There's Any Justice'

8. **Green Day**
'Boulevard of Broken Dreams'

9. **Girls Aloud**
'I'll Stand by You'

10. **Morrissey**
'I Have Forgiven Jesus'

MANY HAPPY CHRISTMAS RETURNS

PART III

Bon Jovi
'Please Come Home for Christmas'
First top-forty peak: 7 (1994)
The number-seven peak of Bon Jovi's seventeenth top-forty hit contributes to their stat of having different singles peak at every position in the Official Chart top ten without ever having a number one. The song was also a number-thirty hit for the Eagles in 1978.

Tom Jones & Cerys
'Baby, It's Cold Outside'
First top-forty peak: 17 (1999)
Originally recorded for the 1949 film *Neptune's Daughter*, when it won the Oscar for Best Original Song, this duet returned to the Official Chart again in 2018, courtesy of Idina Menzel and Michael Bublé, whose cover reached number thirty-nine.

Andy Williams
'It's the Most Wonderful Time of the Year'
First top-forty peak: 21 (2007)
This 1963 recording wasn't released as a single until 2007 when it soundtracked a seasonal TV advert. It has since become a regular visitor to the December chart, reaching a new number-seventeen peak in 2017.

Chris Rea
'Driving Home for Christmas'
First top-forty peak: 33 (2007)
Originally released in 1988 (when it only peaked at number fifty-three), this favourite has since made ten visits to the top forty, beginning in 2007, including a 2020 number-eleven placement. It was also the only solo top-forty hit for 2010 *X Factor* finalist Stacey Solomon, whose cover peaked at number twenty-seven.

Gabriella Cilmi
'Warm This Winter'
First top-forty peak: 22 (2008)
The third of four top-forty hits for Gabriella, this song was originally a 1962 number forty-eight for Connie Francis, who topped the Official Chart twice in 1958 with 'Who's Sorry Now?' and 'Stupid Cupid', as well as gracing our 1960 Christmas top ten with 'My Heart Has a Mind of Its Own'.

George Michael
'December Song (I Dreamed of Christmas)'
First top-forty peak: 14 (2009)
Originally a free download on George's website to thank fans who had bought 'Last Christmas' twenty-five years earlier, this single was also released in a special Christmas card edition, complete with envelope but no stamp.

Pet Shop Boys
'It Doesn't Often Snow at Christmas'
First top-forty peak: 40 (2009)
There are lots of opportunities to mention our 1987 Christmas number-one act, not least this 1997 fan-club recording, which was eventually released as a single in 2009, backed by a cover of Madness's 'My Girl'.

Katy Perry
'Cozy Little Christmas'
First top-forty peak: 23 (2019)
This single has had three separate visits to the top forty so far, culminating in a peak at number twenty-two on its second attempt, though it is not to be confused with Dolly Parton and Michael Bublé's festive single, 'Cuddle Up, Cozy Down Christmas'.

Darlene Love
'Christmas (Baby, Please Come Home)'
First top-forty peak: 22 (2016)
Originally recorded for the 1963 album *A Christmas Gift for You from Phil Spector*, this version first made the Official Chart in 2016, though a 2011 cover by Michael Bublé (again) had peaked at number forty-seven.

Dean Martin
'Let It Snow! Let It Snow! Let It Snow!'
First top-forty peak: 37 (2020)
Dean first recorded this song in 1959 for his album *A Winter Romance*, though he recorded a second version in 1966 for his *Christmas Album*. A Frank Sinatra version from 1950 peaked at fifty-six in 2020, too.

Kylie Minogue
'Santa Baby'
First top-forty peak: 38 (2017)
First released in 2007, Kylie's cover only reached number seventy-six. Though it first broke into the top forty in 2017, it actually achieved its best position so far (number thirty-one) in 2020, at the same time as Eartha Kitt's 1953 original reached number fifty-five.

José Feliciano
'Feliz Navidad'
First top-forty peak: 40 (2020)
Originally recorded by the Puerto Rican songwriter in 1970, this bilingual single only broke into the top forty in the final week of 2020 – fifty-two years after José made his Official Chart debut with a number-six cover of the Doors' 'Light My Fire'.

Official Christmas Number 1

2005

SHAYNE WARD
'THAT'S MY GOAL'

FOLLOW-UP SINGLE: 'NO PROMISES'
APRIL 2006

WEEKS AT NUMBER ONE
4

HIGHEST CHART POSITION
2

At the risk of giving too much away, 2005 begins a period of considerable success in the Christmas top ten for *X Factor* contestants, starting with the winner of the second series, Shayne, who must have been plotting his overnight success since he reached the final thirty of *Popstars: The Rivals* in 2002. (Steve Brookstein, series 1 winner, also went to number one, though his debut single was released after Christmas.)

In 2005's *X Factor* final, Shayne saw off competition from duo Journey South (who, rather inexplicably, have a number-one album but no top-forty hits) and Andy Abraham (who made his own attempt on the Christmas top ten with the 2006 number eighteen 'December Brings Me Back to You'). 'That's My Goal' entered the Official Chart at number one on Christmas Day, with first-week sales of almost 750,000 – more than the rest of the top forty combined.

23 January: Mark 'Bez' Berry of the Happy Mondays wins the third series of *Celebrity Big Brother* |

'That's My Goal' was co-written by Swede Jörgen Elofsson and is one of his eight Official Chart chart-toppers. His other seven comprise four for Westlife ('If I Let You Go', 'Fool Again, 'My Love' and 'Unbreakable') and one each for Will Young, Gareth Gates and Leona Lewis ('Evergreen', 'Anyone of Us' and 'A Moment Like This').

Shayne went on to have a further five top-forty hits and a number-one album before opting to join our still rather exclusive 'Christmas number-one stars who have appeared in *Coronation Street*' club (travel back to 1983 for further details). Incidentally, Shayne's character on the soap, Aidan Connor, was the cousin of Michelle Connor, played by fellow talent-show winner Kym Marsh of Hear'Say.

NUMBER TWO
NIZLOPI
'JCB SONG'

We have come very close to sounding our 'one-hit wonder' klaxon again, but – by dint of one week spent at number ninety-one with their follow-up single, 'Girls' – Warwickshire duo Luke Concannon and John Parker can walk away with their heads held high.

'JCB Song' had originally been released six months earlier but

2005
CHRISTMAS TOP TEN

1. **Shayne Ward**
   'That's My Goal'
2. **Nizlopi**
   'JCB Song'
3. **The Pogues feat. Kirsty MacColl**
   'Fairytale of New York'
4. **Westlife feat. Diana Ross**
   'When You Tell Me That You Love Me'
5. **Eminem**
   'When I'm Gone'
6. **Crazy Frog**
   'Jingle Bells'/'U Can't Touch This'
7. **Pussycat Dolls**
   'Stickwitu'
8. **Madonna**
   'Hung Up'
9. **Girls Aloud**
   'See the Day'
10. **Coldplay**
    'Talk'

failed to chart. However, support from radio and an attention-grabbing animated video (YouTube had launched the previous February) prompted a re-issue in December that saw the single enter the Official Chart at number one. Though 'JCB Song' achieved sales of more than 80,000 copies in its first week and almost double that in its second, this was nowhere near enough to ward off Shayne.

2 July: Pink Floyd reunite with Roger Waters for the Live 8 concert in London

Official Christmas Number 1

2006

LEONA LEWIS 'A MOMENT LIKE THIS'

FOLLOW-UP SINGLE: 'BLEEDING LOVE'
NOVEMBER 2007

WEEKS AT NUMBER ONE
4

HIGHEST CHART POSITION
1

If 2005 changed how the British public chose their Christmas number one, 2006 would mark a significant shift in how they bought it. On the evening of Saturday 16 December, Leona triumphed over Ray Quinn as the winner of the third series of *The X Factor*, with her debut single available to download immediately after the show, though not released on CD until the following Wednesday. 'A Moment Like This' finished the week with more than 570,000 sales, with downloads accounting for almost 25 per cent of the total – a big enough contribution to claim the top spot without the need for physical sales. Within two weeks, it became the second best-selling single of the year, beaten only by Gnarls Barkley's 'Crazy', though Leona's follow-up, 'Bleeding Love', would take the title in 2007.

11 March: James Blunt becomes the first British artist to top the US *Billboard* Hot 100 since Elton John

'A Moment Like This' had been the debut single of 2002 *American Idol* winner Kelly Clarkson, reaching number eleven in the US, but confined to her debut album in the UK. Leona's ability to release a cover that outperforms the original was evidenced again by 'Run'. While the Snow Patrol original reached number five in 2004, Leona's version went on to spend two weeks at number one, as well as making an appearance in our 2008 Christmas top ten. She will return to our Yuletide chart once more in 2013 with 'One More Sleep', taken from her *Christmas, with Love* album.

NUMBER TWO
TAKE THAT
'PATIENCE'

Picking up from where 'How Deep Is Your Love' left off in 1996, 'Patience' became Take That's ninth number one in 2006. It was taken from *Beautiful World*, the recently reformed band's first new album in eleven years and their first as a quartet (without Robbie).

Entering the Official Chart at number four on 19 November, the single began its four-week run at the top a week later, displacing the not particularly festive 'Smack That' by Akon featuring Eminem. While 'Patience' may have missed out on

2006
CHRISTMAS TOP TEN

1 Leona Lewis
'A Moment Like This'

2 Take That
'Patience'

3 McFly
'Sorry's Not Good Enough'

4 Girls Aloud
'I Think We're Alone Now'

5 Cascada
'Truly Madly Deeply'

6 The Pogues feat. Kirsty MacColl
'Fairytale of New York'

7 Cliff Richard
'21st Century Christmas'/'Move It'

8 Booty Luv
'Boogie 2Nite'

9 Akon feat. Eminem
'Smack That'

10 Chris Cornell
'You Know My Name'

the Christmas number-one spot, it had the satisfaction of winning British Single of the Year at the BRIT Awards the following February.

Official Christmas Number 1

2007
LEON JACKSON
'WHEN YOU BELIEVE'

FOLLOW-UP SINGLE: 'DON'T CALL THIS LOVE' OCTOBER 2008

WEEKS AT NUMBER ONE 3

HIGHEST CHART POSITION 3

After Leon saw off Welsh singer Rhydian Roberts to win the fourth series of *The X Factor*, he released a cover of 'When You Believe', originally written for the animated musical film *The Prince of Egypt* and a number-four hit for Mariah Carey and Whitney Houston in 1998. While viewing figures for the TV talent contest were up, sales of the winner's single were less than half of our 2006 Christmas number one, though the shift in buying habits

continued, with downloads counting for almost 30 per cent of the total – once again, enough to capture the top spot outright.

In the *X Factor* final, Leon also covered 'White Christmas' – number six in our very first Christmas top ten back in 1952 – and duetted with Kylie Minogue on 'Better the Devil You Know'. (Kylie's original version reached number two in May 1990 and a cover by Steps claimed a place in our 1999 Christmas top ten.) Everything seemed rosy when

2 January: Des O'Connor succeeds Des Lynam as presenter of Channel 4 quiz show *Countdown* | **17 March:**

Leon's second single, 'Don't Call This Love', charted at number three in October 2008 and his debut album, *Right Now*, reached number four the following month. However, his third single, 'Creative', only crept in for one week at number ninety-four and then his record label dropped him the following spring.

Though obviously not the most successful Jackson to have graced the top forty, he can take some consolation in being the biggest Leon. The somewhat limited competition comes from Leon Haywood (number twelve with 'Don't Push It Don't Force It' in 1980) and Leon Bridges (number eight with 'Coming Home' in 2015).

NUMBER TWO
EVA CASSIDY & KATIE MELUA 'WHAT A WONDERFUL WORLD'

This posthumous hit was the only top-forty entry for Eva, who died in 1996, aged just thirty-three. Eva and Katie's cover of Louis Armstrong's 1968 number one had topped the Official Chart the week before and was the work of producer Mike Batt. Mike had overseen Georgian-born Katie's five previous top-forty entries and he donned a furry suit for an appearance in our 1974 Christmas top ten with the Wombles and 'Wombling Merry Christmas'.

2007
CHRISTMAS TOP TEN

1 Leon Jackson
'When You Believe'

2 Eva Cassidy & Katie Melua
'What a Wonderful World'

3 Leona Lewis
'Bleeding Love'

4 The Pogues feat. Kirsty MacColl
'Fairytale of New York'

5 Soulja Boy Tell'em
'Crank That (Soulja Boy)'

6 Mariah Carey
'All I Want for Christmas Is You'

7 Take That
'Rule the World'

8 Mark Ronson feat. Amy Winehouse
'Valerie'

9 Girls Aloud
'Call the Shots'

10 Timbaland feat. One Republic
'Apologize'

A charity project in aid of the British Red Cross and championed by Radio 2's Terry Wogan, 'What a Wonderful World' bucked the trend towards digital downloads quite convincingly, with 97 per cent of its first-week total generated by sales of the CD single, which was exclusive to a certain UK supermarket. (Clue: the name rhymes with 'al fresco').

The rebuilt Wembley Stadium in London opens | 8 June: Adele makes her TV debut on *Later… with Jools Holland*

Official Christmas Number 1

2008

ALEXANDRA BURKE
'HALLELUJAH'

FOLLOW-UP SINGLE: 'BAD BOYS'
OCTOBER 2009

WEEKS AT NUMBER ONE
3

HIGHEST CHART POSITION
1

We reach a time in our Christmas chart-topper story when *The X Factor* is fully established as king- or queen-maker. However, 2008 was also an important tipping point, as it was the first year that downloads of the Christmas number-one single exceeded sales on CD.

Following Alexandra's victory, we once more had two versions of the same song in the Christmas top ten – but this time, unlike the previous

occurrence ('Wonderwall', 1995), neither version was the original. (That said, interest in the 24-year-old ballad did result in the original Leonard Cohen recording entering the Official Chart down at number thirty-six.) We have to go right back to 1957 to find another example of the same song occupying the top two spots: Guy Mitchell and Tommy Steele's competing versions of 'Singing the Blues' (both of which had a turn at number one).

---

22 May: Construction work begins on the London Stadium for the 2012 Olympic Games | 15 September:

With 576,000 sales in her first week, Alexandra not only replaced former *X Factor* winner Leona Lewis at number one, but also claimed the best-selling single of 2008 after just two weeks. In January 2009, she passed the million sales mark, making her the first British female solo artist to do so. However, to add a little intrigue, 'Hallelujah' is still only the second biggest-selling *X Factor* winner's single…

Fast-forward ten months to Cheryl Cole knocking 'Bad Boys' by former protégée Alexandra off the top spot with her second solo single, 'Fight for This Love'. The Girls-Aloud-singer-turned-*X-Factor*-judge remained at number one for two weeks until *X Factor* 2008 runners-up JLS replaced her with their second number one, 'Everybody in Love'.

NUMBER TWO
JEFF BUCKLEY
'HALLELUJAH'

Inspired by a version recorded by former Velvet Underground member John Cale for the Leonard Cohen tribute album *I'm Your Fan*, Jeff Buckley's version of 'Hallelujah' had to wait thirteen years before it charted, though the singer didn't live to see it happen. Jeff drowned while swimming in the Mississippi River in May 1997.

2008
CHRISTMAS TOP TEN

1 **Alexandra Burke**
'Hallelujah'

2 **Jeff Buckley**
'Hallelujah'

3 **Leona Lewis**
'Run'

4 **Beyoncé**
'If I Were a Boy'

5 **Geraldine**
'Once Upon a Christmas Song'

6 **James Morrison feat. Nelly Furtado**
'Broken Strings'

7 **Kings of Leon**
'Use Somebody'

8 **Beyoncé**
'Listen'

9 **Take That**
'Greatest Day'

10 **Britney Spears**
'Womanizer'

Not released as a CD single, its appearance on the chart – entirely driven by downloads – shows not only a change in buying habits, but also the growing power of social media to focus a campaign. This may have marked the first stirrings of an *X Factor* backlash, too, though come back next year for more on that subject…

Children's TV drama series *Grange Hill* ends after thirty years and 601 episodes

2009

RAGE AGAINST THE MACHINE
'KILLING IN THE NAME'

WEEKS AT NUMBER ONE
1

After four years of *X Factor* domination, an online campaign was launched by Essex couple Jon and Tracy Morter in a bid to prevent the 2009 winner claiming the Christmas number-one title. Their weapon of choice was the sweary anthem 'Killing in the Name' by American rock band Rage Against the Machine and they described the campaign as 'one of those little silly ideas that make you laugh', though Simon Cowell, *X Factor* judge and record label boss, branded it 'stupid'. That didn't seem to discourage people, as 'Killing in the Name' was downloaded more

than half a million times, eventually beating Joe McElderry's 'The Climb' by more than 50,000 sales. (Simon later congratulated the Morters on a successful campaign, which BBC News rather bizarrely compared to crooner Engelbert Humperdinck ending the Beatles' run of eleven consecutive number ones.)

In the sixteen-year gap between 'Killing in the Name' making its 1993 Official Chart debut (when Radio 1

---

6 January: The last of Woolworths' 813 UK stores closes | 22 February: *Slumdog Millionaire* wins eight Oscars

DJ Bruno Brookes accidentally played the uncensored version on his top-forty countdown) and topping the Official Chart, Rage Against the Machine had five further top-forty entries, though none hung around for more than two weeks. In June 2010, the band celebrated their belated success with a free concert in Finsbury Park, London, during which they handed a cheque for £162,000 to Jon and Tracy. Royalties from the single plus donations from fans went to homeless charity Shelter.

A 2011 campaign from the same couple saw Nirvana's 'Smells Like Teen Spirit' re-enter the chart at number eleven, while the same tactics also took AC/DC's 'Highway to Hell' to number four in 2013.

NUMBER TWO
JOE McELDERRY
'THE CLIMB'

After the world of pop tilted on its axis, order was restored the following week when 'The Climb' (originally recorded by Christmas 2018 top-ten artist Miley Cyrus for *Hannah Montana: The Movie*) sold 195,000 copies and claimed the number-one spot. Joe had just one more top-forty hit ('Ambitions', 2010) and his Official Chart career was surpassed by that of 2009 *X Factor* runner-up Olly Murs, who has had four number ones.

2009
CHRISTMAS TOP TEN

1 **Rage Against the Machine**
'Killing in the Name'

2 **Joe McElderry**
'The Climb'

3 **Lady Gaga**
'Bad Romance'

4 **Peter Kay's Animated All Star Band**
'The Official BBC Children in Need Medley'

5 **3OH!3 feat. Katy Perry**
'Starstrukk'

6 **Robbie Williams**
'You Know Me'

7 **Cheryl Cole**
'3 Words'

8 **Rihanna**
'Russian Roulette'

9 **Journey**
'Don't Stop Believin''

10 **Black Eyed Peas**
'Meet Me Halfway'

In 2011, Joe won the talent show *Popstar to Operastar* and released a collection of Yuletide favourites on his *Classic Christmas* album. Three years later, he won yet another reality TV show – winter sports series *The Jump* – having competed alongside Pussycat Dolls singer Kimberly Wyatt and Ritchie Neville from 5ive.

at the eighty-first Academy Awards | 22 August: Oasis play their last-ever gig at Weston Park, Stafford

SOME OLDE CURIOSITIES
PART III

Fat Les
'Naughty Christmas (Goblin in the Office)'
Chart peak: 21 (1998)
This was the second of three top-forty hits for the band that comprised actor Keith Allen, artist Damien Hirst and Blur's Alex James. Their debut single, 'Vindaloo', spent three weeks at number two, kept from the top spot by 'Three Lions '98' by Baddiel, Skinner and the Lightning Seeds.

Cocteau Twins
'Frosty the Snowman'
Chart peak: 58 (1993)
The only Official Chart version of this Christmas classic came from the Cocteau Twins, a trio whose 1984 top-forty hit, 'Pearly-Dewdrops' Drops', was voted the second best single of the year by John Peel's listeners on Radio 1.

Cyndi Lauper
'Christmas Conga'
Released: 1998 (did not chart)
If her '80s hit 'Girls Just Want to Have Fun' wasn't enough to get your party swinging, Cyndi also recorded this festive gem, which includes the lyrics, 'Bonga, bonga, bonga, do the Christmas conga!'

Roy 'Chubby' Brown
'Rockin' Good Christmas'
Chart peak: 51 (1996)
This was the only remotely radio-friendly track from Roy's album *Fat Out of Hell*. It came after 1995's 'Who the F**k is Alice?' went to number three for Smokie featuring Roy.

Tweenies
'I Believe in Christmas'
Chart peak: 9 (2001)
This was the fourth of five top-forty hits for the CBeebies pre-school favourites, though their overt attempt to get to number one with a debut single called 'No. 1' failed when it stalled at number five.

The Wurzels
'Come On Santa'
Chart peak: 98 (2001)
This was a disappointing chart peak for the Wurzels after a re-issue of their 1976 chart-topper, 'The Combine Harvester', took them back into the top forty. Things got slightly better in 2002, though, when their take on Oasis's 'Don't Look Back in Anger' reached number fifty-nine.

Jane McDonald
'Cruise into Christmas'
Chart peak: 10 (1998)
Although this was Jane's sole top-forty single, her high profile helped her land eight top-forty albums between 1998 and 2020.

Bo' Selecta!
'Proper Crimbo'
Chart peak: 4 (2003)
This was the first of two Official Chart entries for comedian Leigh Francis (see our 2004 Christmas top ten for the other). Leigh also co-hosted the 2011 game show *Sing If You Can* (alongside *X Factor* finalist Stacey Solomon) and made a brief appearance in the 2019 Elton John biopic, *Rocketman*.

Fast Food Rockers
'I Love Christmas'
Chart peak: 25 (2003)
This was the third of three top-forty hits for the UK trio, whose Official Chart debut, 'Fast Food Song', spent two weeks at number two, only denied the top spot by Evanescence with 'Bring Me to Life'.

Crazy Frog
'Jingle Bells'
Chart peak: 5 (2005)
This novelty act matched the aforementioned Tweenies' five top-forty hits, but also scored a number one with their debut single, 'Axel F'. Their chart-topping cover bettered the 1985 Harold Faltermeyer original, which had stalled at number two.

Ricky Tomlinson
'Christmas My A*se!'
Chart peak: 25 (2006)
A spin-off from BBC TV sitcom *The Royle Family*, this was the second top-forty hit for actor Ricky Tomlinson. His first, 'Are You Lookin' at Me?', reached number twenty-eight in 2001 and included additional vocals from Noddy Holder of Christmas chart-toppers Slade.

Geraldine
'Once Upon a Christmas Song'
Chart peak: 5 (2008)
Peter Kay now boasts three chart-toppers (one in the guise of *Phoenix Nights*' Brian Potter) plus three top-forty singles as Geraldine McQueen. This festive hit was co-written with Gary Barlow for the parody talent show *Britain's Got the Pop Factor...*

Cast of *The Only Way is Essex*
'Last Christmas'
Chart peak: 33 (2011)
This is the least successful of the three top-forty cover versions of this song; the other two were by Whigfield (number twenty-one in 1995) and Crazy Frog (number sixteen in 2006). Visit our entry for Christmas 2020 to see how Wham!'s original 1984 version eventually fared.

Eddie Stobart Truckers
'12 Days of Christmas'
Chart peak: 47 (2012)
And here we have another TV spin-off, this time from a Channel 5 series following the fortunes of the eponymous haulage company. To its credit, this release did better than the Wurzels' 1995 number ninety-three, 'I Want to Be an Eddie Stobart Driver'.

WELCOME TO THE '10s

And so we arrive at the 2010s – the decade in which the rebellious youths of our story so far became mature elder statespersons and their contributions to soundtracking our lives, shaping our charts and boosting our economy saw them conferred with honorific titles. So arise Sir Cliff Richard, Dame Shirley Bassey, Sir Tom Jones, Sir Van Morrison, Sir Barry Gibb, Dame Olivia Newton-John, Sir Ray Davies, Sir Mick Jagger, Sir Elton John, Sir Paul McCartney, Sir Ringo Starr, Sir Tommy Steele and Sir Rod Stewart.

Pop music, once considered a passing fad, was cemented as big business: chart hits became musicals, the musicals became films, the films had soundtracks, and the soundtracks went back into the chart. Adverts, football, athletics, anniversaries, opening events, closing events – no occasion was complete without an official (or unofficial) single. Rude-boys-turned-national-treasures Madness played on the roof of Buckingham Palace, while the music of *Doctor Who* was deemed worthy of a performance at the Proms. In 2012, celebrations to mark the sixtieth anniversary of the Official Singles Chart included a parliamentary reception attended by number-one acts Sandie Shaw, Boney M. and Soft Cell's Marc Almond, as well as chart-show hosts past and present in the form of Tony Blackburn and Jameela Jamil.

Sadly, the advanced years of the Official Chart meant an increasing number of pop pioneers and former number-one artists were taken from us this decade. Music's particular *annus horribilis* was 2016, which saw the passing of David Bowie, Prince, Sir George Martin, Greg Lake and George Michael, among others. The decade also claimed the lives of younger talents Amy Winehouse and Swedish DJ Avicii, who both died before they reached thirty.

While the '00s had the most number-one singles of any ten-year period (282, compared to 169 in the '70s), the introduction of streaming figures to the Official Chart in 2014 would, in the words of Bucks Fizz, 'speed it up' and 'slow it down', with songs entering the chart quicker than before and hanging around longer. The first half of the decade averaged thirty-four different number-one singles per year, but this slowed to sixteen in the second half as the impact of younger listeners favouring streaming over radio was felt.

Now that it was possible to send high-quality music files across the internet, there was no need for collaborators to be in the same country, let alone the same studio, so the number of 'featured' artists proliferated. Indeed, the first half of the '10s were peak 'featuring' years, with sixty-four out of 168 number-one singles (or 38 per cent) involving one artist featuring another. This spirit of cooperation also contributed to a blurring of traditional music genres: pop embraced hip-hop (Olly Murs featuring Flo Rida) and hung out with grime (Ed Sheeran featuring Stormzy); electro cuddled up with R&B (Daft Punk featuring Pharrell Williams) and Latin pop got cosy with Latin rap (Jennifer Lopez featuring Pitbull);

indie made friends with soul (fun. featuring Janelle Monáe) and rap stepped out with country (Lil Nas X featuring Billy Ray Cyrus), as did pop (Bebe Rexha featuring Florida Georgia Line). It was almost as though pop was short for 'popular'.

The decade's advance in technology, change in reader habits and decline in print advertising resulted in the *New Musical Express* – the source of our very first Official Chart – announcing that it would discontinue its physical edition and concentrate on its online version. Unfortunately, the waning circulation of the music press made it difficult for other publications to continue and, having lost *Smash Hits* and *Melody Maker* the previous decade, we said goodbye to *Q* magazine in 2020.

There was a downturn in number-one film themes, too, with the notable exception of Pharrell Williams' 'Happy' from *Despicable Me 2* (the best-selling single of 2014). Sam Smith's 'Writing's on the Wall' from *Spectre* also became the first James Bond theme to reach number one in the UK and the second to win an Oscar for Best Original Song – hot on the heels of Adele, who won for 'Skyfall' in 2012.

Meanwhile, some of the attention turned to adverts for John Lewis department stores. Their annual seasonal campaign became a new source of anticipation as well as a contender for the Christmas number-one slot, with Gabrielle Aplin's 'The Power of Love' (2012) and Lily Allen's 'Somewhere Only We Know' (2013) both hitting the top spot in December, though peaking a little too early to merit a spread in our book.

Elsewhere on TV, *All Together Now*, *The Big Reunion* and *Must Be the Music* provided brief diversions, though our Christmas number-one story is all the better for the military wives assembled by Gareth Malone in the 2011 series of *The Choir*. It's also only fair we doff our cap to ITV's occasional series *The Nation's Favourite…*, which devoted a 2012 episode to Christmas songs. (The nation chose the Pogues over any of our actual Christmas number ones.)

The influence of musical behemoth *The X Factor* dimmed a little in comparison to the previous decade, but then there was an awful lot to live up to. It started well in 2010, with the show's seventh series attracting its highest ever average audience, but half the viewers had moved on by 2018. In December 2011, the *X Factor* finalists were replaced at number one by the 2009 runner-up Olly Murs, who made way for 2011 winners Little Mix the following week. By the end of 2020, the show had generated an impressive total of forty-three UK number-one hits, while Little Mix, One Direction, Olly Murs and JLS were unavoidable presences during the '10s. In 2019, the show was 'rested' with no news of when it might return.

Perhaps we had rediscovered the true meaning of Christmas? If we include 2020, seven of the past eleven Christmas number ones have been charity singles, with another eleven chart-topping fundraising projects nestled between them.

However, instant access to festive favourites via streaming and voice-activated speakers actually gave the 2020 Christmas chart a very familiar look: five of the top ten had been there before (including two former Christmas number ones) and seven of the song titles included the word 'Christmas'. The nation was wrapping itself in the comforting glow of nostalgia.

'Does your granny always tell you the old songs are the best?' Perhaps she was right.

Let's find out…

2010

MATT CARDLE
'WHEN WE COLLIDE'

FOLLOW-UP SINGLE: 'RUN FOR YOUR LIFE'
OCTOBER 2011

WEEKS AT NUMBER ONE
3

HIGHEST CHART POSITION
6

The 2010 Christmas number one went to 27-year-old Matt, yet another *X Factor* winner, who beat competition from Rebecca Ferguson (three solo top-forty hits plus a credit on our 2012 Christmas number one) and a boy band named One Direction (four number-one singles and four number-one albums). All three acts appeared on the *X Factor* finalists' charity single – a version of David Bowie's 'Heroes'

– that spent two weeks at number one at the beginning of December.

'When We Collide' sold 439,000 copies in its first week and would become the fourth best-selling *X Factor* winner's single and the third to sell a million. It was also the second best-selling single of 2010, finishing behind Eminem's 'Love the Way You Lie', featuring Rihanna, who Matt rubbed shoulders with during

---

1 January: Actor David Tennant makes his final appearance in the title role of *Doctor Who* | **7 March:**

the *X Factor* final when they sang a duet of her 2006 number-two hit 'Unfaithful'.

Matt's single was actually a cover of 'Many of Horror' by Scottish rock band Biffy Clyro. Their original version had reached number twenty earlier in the year, but renewed interest and a to-be-expected online campaign saw it re-chart at number eight. This re-entry gave Biffy Clyro their longest top-forty spell (nine weeks), but not their highest-placed single – that honour goes to 'Mountains', which peaked at number five in September 2008.

In August 2013, Matt teamed up with ex-Spice Girl Melanie C – another Christmas number-one singer and fellow member of the million-seller club – for 'Loving You', which reached number fourteen and was his third and final top-forty single.

NUMBER TWO
RIHANNA FEAT. DRAKE
'WHAT'S MY NAME'

'What's My Name' waited patiently at number two for three weeks before replacing Matt at the top of the Official Chart in January 2011. It was one of six top-forty hits in 2010 for Barbadian Rihanna and one of three for Canadian Drake, giving the former her fifth number one and the latter his first.

2010
CHRISTMAS TOP TEN

1. Matt Cardle
'When We Collide'

2. Rihanna feat. Drake
'What's My Name'

3. The Trashmen
'Surfin' Bird'

4. Black Eyed Peas
'The Time (Dirty Bit)'

5. Ellie Goulding
'Your Song'

6. Take That
'The Flood'

7. Rihanna
'Only Girl (In the World)'

8. Biffy Clyro
'Many of Horror'

9. Willow
'Whip My Hair'

10. Michael Jackson feat. Akon
'Hold My Hand'

While none can compete with Rihanna's forty-plus top-forty hits, other pop ambassadors from the Caribbean island include Mark Morrison (number one with 'Return of the Mack' in 1996), Cover Drive (number one with 'Twilight' in 2012) and Shontelle, whose 2010 number nine, 'Impossible', was covered by James Arthur for his debut single. (More on James later…)

Kathryn Bigelow becomes the first female winner of a Best Director Oscar

Official Christmas Number 1

2011

MILITARY WIVES WITH GARETH MALONE
'WHEREVER YOU ARE'

WEEKS AT NUMBER ONE
1

HIGHEST CHART POSITION
42

GARETH MALONE'S FOLLOW-UP SINGLE: 'WAKE ME UP'
NOVEMBER 2004

And so to the sixtieth Christmas number one – that honour fell to the Military Wives. The choir, which comprised the wives and girlfriends of serving personnel from two British Army bases in Devon, was coached by choirmaster Gareth Malone for the fourth series of BBC TV programme *The Choir*. Their debut single, 'Wherever You Are', featured extracts from the wives' letters set to music by Welsh composer Paul Mealor.

First-week sales of 556,000 were greater than the rest of the top ten combined and, bucking the digital trend, included more than 400,000 sales on CD single. Proceeds from 'Wherever You Are' were donated to the Royal British Legion and the Soldiers, Sailors, Airmen and Families Association.

The year's now-commonplace 'let's stop the *X Factor* winner

23 July: Singer and songwriter Amy Winehouse dies, aged twenty-seven | 6 September: PJ Harvey's

getting to number one' efforts included Radio 1 DJ Chris Moyles' campaign centred around the 1960 single 'Dominick the Donkey' by Lou Monte. Dominick became the first *Equus africanus asinus* to grace the Christmas top ten since 'Little Donkey' by Nina & Frederik in 1960 (if we ignore a 2009 cameo appearance by Muffin the Mule in Peter Kay's Animated All Star Band). Vlogger Alex Day also made a bid for the top with 'Forever Yours' (the first of his three top-forty hits), though the single fell from number four to number 112 a week later, setting a new record for the biggest drop in Official Chart history.

NUMBER TWO
LITTLE MIX
'CANNONBALL'

The first group to win *The X Factor*, Little Mix have gone on to become one of the most successful acts ever to emerge from the show and, in 2020, 'Sweet Melody' became their fifth number one.

The girls' cover of Damien Rice's 2003 number nine was the only other entry in the 2010 Christmas top ten to be available on the declining CD-single format, though the additional 65,000 sales more than justified this. Little Mix's competition in the final of the eighth series was Marcus Collins, who

2011
CHRISTMAS TOP TEN

1. **Military Wives with Gareth Malone**
'Wherever You Are'

2. **Little Mix**
'Cannonball'

3. **Lou Monte**
'Dominick the Donkey'

4. **Alex Day**
'Forever Yours'

5. **Coldplay**
'Paradise'

6. **Olly Murs**
'Dance with Me Tonight'

7. **Flo Rida**
'Good Feeling'

8. **Lloyd feat. Andre 3000 & Lil Wayne**
'Dedication to My Ex (Miss That)'

9. **Avicii**
'Levels'

10. **Rihanna feat. Calvin Harris**
'We Found Love'

reached number nine in March 2012 with his cover of the White Stripes' 'Seven Nation Army', and Amelia Lily, who hit an impressive number-two peak with her debut single, 'You Bring Me Joy', but was kept from the top spot by 'Hall of Fame' by the Script featuring will.i.am.

album *Let England Shake* scoops the Mercury Music Prize, making her the first person to win twice

2012

JUSTICE COLLECTIVE
'HE AIN'T HEAVY, HE'S MY BROTHER'

WEEKS AT NUMBER ONE

1

of former Liverpool and Everton FC footballers.

One of the closer Christmas number-one contests of recent years saw victory for the Justice Collective with their cover of the Hollies' 1969 single 'He Ain't Heavy, He's My Brother'. Proceeds were donated to families of the ninety-six Liverpool FC supporters who died at Hillsborough Stadium, Sheffield, on 15 April 1989. The collective included Paul McCartney, Gerry Marsden, Holly Johnson, Melanie C, Robbie Williams and Shane MacGowan of the Pogues, as well as the strings of the Liverpool Philharmonic Orchestra, a gospel choir and a 'Cats Choir' made up

It took the Hollies' version nineteen years to get to number one (the single was re-issued in 1988 after being used in a TV advert), but the Justice Collective got their cover to the top in just seven days, with first-week sales of 270,000 copies.

A related 2012 campaign also saw Gerry and the Pacemakers 1963 number one 'You'll Never Walk Alone' re-enter the chart, peaking at number twelve on 16 September. The song, originally written for the Rodgers and Hammerstein musical *Carousel*, topped the Official Chart for a second time in 1985 when

7 July: Opening ceremony of the Summer Olympic Games in London (Great Britain would go on to win

charity supergroup the Crowd recorded a version to raise funds for victims of the Bradford City stadium fire. Once again, Gerry Marsden and Paul McCartney were among those lending their talent and support to the cover. In 2020, a third chart-topping version of 'You'll Never Walk Alone' was released – this time by Michael Ball and Captain Sir Tom Moore – and its proceeds were added to the £33 million Captain Tom raised for NHS charities during the coronavirus crisis. At the age of 100, Captain Tom became the oldest person ever to score an Official Chart number one.

NUMBER TWO
JAMES ARTHUR
'IMPOSSIBLE'

After topping the Official Chart on 16 December, the winner of the ninth series of *The X Factor* dropped down to second place for a week before returning to the top for two more. With sales totalling almost 900,000 copies, James finished 2012 with the year's fifth best-selling single ('Somebody That I Used to Know' by Gotye featuring Kimbra came out on top) and went on to become the fourth winner of the talent contest to sell a million copies of their debut single. In 2017, 'Impossible' finally overtook Alexandra Burke's 'Hallelujah' to be crowned biggest *X Factor* winner's song.

2012
CHRISTMAS TOP TEN

1. **Justice Collective**
   'He Ain't Heavy, He's My Brother'

2. **James Arthur**
   'Impossible'

3. **will.i.am feat. Britney Spears**
   'Scream & Shout'

4. **Rihanna feat. Mikky Ekko**
   'Stay'

5. **Bruno Mars**
   'Locked Out of Heaven'

6. **Psy**
   'Gangnam Style'

7. **Olly Murs feat. Flo Rida**
   'Troublemaker'

8. **Taylor Swift**
   'I Knew You Were Trouble'

9. **Gabrielle Aplin**
   'The Power of Love'

10. **Rihanna**
    'Diamonds'

Partnering with Dalton Harris (a later *X Factor* winner), James would have his tenth top-forty hit in December 2018 with a number-four cover of 'The Power of Love'. A previous cover of that same song (originally by Frankie Goes to Hollywood) also appears in this year's Christmas top ten, courtesy of Gabrielle Aplin's recording for the seasonal John Lewis advertising campaign.

twenty-nine gold medals) | 6 November: Actor and singer Clive Dunn dies, aged ninety-two

2013

SAM BAILEY
'SKYSCRAPER'

FOLLOW-UP SINGLE: 'COMPASS'
MARCH 2014

WEEKS AT NUMBER ONE
1

HIGHEST CHART POSITION
DID NOT CHART

On 15 December, Sam – a former prison guard from Leicester – beat Nicholas McDonald and Luke Friend to win the tenth series of *The X Factor*. Her debut single was a cover of 'Skyscraper' – a number thirty-two hit for Demi Lovato in 2012 that re-charted at number seven following Sam's first performance of it. Although Sam's success returned the TV talent show to the top of the Christmas chart after two years of second-place finishes, first-

week sales of 149,000 made this single the lowest-selling Christmas number one for more than ten years.

In March 2014, runner-up Nicholas released his debut single, 'Answerphone', which limped to number seventy-three, while Luke's moment in the sun came in April 2015 when 'Hole in My Heart' reached number forty. With a loud blast of our 'one-hit wonder' klaxon, we can reveal that all three *X Factor*

7 July: Andy Murray becomes the first British male to win Wimbledon since 1936, beating Novak Djokovic in

2013 finalists are still awaiting a follow-up Official Chart hit.

December 2013 also saw irate keyboard warriors and fans of all things rock getting behind AC/DC's 1979 single 'Highway to Hell' in an attempt to derail Sam's bid for the top spot. Though the Australian rockers can boast four number-one albums and twenty-one top-forty singles, their number-four peak here is the band's only entry in the UK top ten to date.

Sam's debut album, *The Power of Love* (named after the song by Jennifer Rush, not Huey Lewis and the News or Frankie Goes to Hollywood), took her to number one, too, and featured duets with Michael Bolton and Pussycat Doll Nicole Scherzinger. A re-issued December 2014 'gift edition' added Sam's versions of five festive favourites, including 'Silent Night' – a Christmas number eight for both Bing Crosby (1952) and Bros (1988).

NUMBER TWO
PHARRELL WILLIAMS
'HAPPY'

By December, Pharrell had already featured on the two biggest number-one hits this year: 'Blurred Lines' by Robin Thicke (also featuring T.I.) and 'Get Lucky' by Daft Punk (also featuring Nile Rodgers).

2013
CHRISTMAS TOP TEN

1 **Sam Bailey**
   'Skyscraper'

2 **Pharrell Williams**
   'Happy'

3 **Leona Lewis**
   'One More Sleep'

4 **AC/DC**
   'Highway to Hell'

5 **Avicii**
   'Hey Brother'

6 **Lily Allen**
   'Somewhere Only We Know'

7 **Ellie Goulding**
   'How Long Will I Love You?'

8 **Jason Derulo**
   'Trumpets'

9 **Eminem feat. Rihanna**
   'The Monster'

10 **One Direction**
   'Story of My Life'

'Happy' – Pharrell's fifteenth top-forty hit and the best-selling single of 2014 – would spend a total of six non-consecutive weeks at number two, interspersed with three spells at number one.

He would have to wait until 2017 for his next chart-topper, 'Feels', on which he shared the credits with Scottish DJ Calvin Harris (ten number ones), Katy Perry (five number ones) and rapper Big Sean (just the one so far).

straight sets | 7 September: Marin Alsop becomes the first woman to conduct the Last Night of the Proms

2014

BEN HAENOW
'SOMETHING I NEED'

FOLLOW-UP SINGLE: 'SECOND HAND HEART'
MARCH 2014

WEEKS AT NUMBER ONE
1

HIGHEST CHART POSITION
21

The seventh and most recent *X Factor* winner to claim the Christmas number-one title, Ben Haenow won the eleventh series, beating Fleur East and Andrea Faustini, and his reward was a cover version of the OneRepublic song 'Something I Need'. It entered the Official Chart at number one, selling 214,000 copies, and, for the first time, audio streams counted towards the total, with 100 streams the equivalent of one download or CD single. That said, the old-fashioned silver disc was still key to Ben's success, with 47,000 of his fans deciding it was something they needed. However, new-fangled streaming did see the original OneRepublic version enter the Official Chart at number seventy-eight, even though it had never been released as a single in the UK.

While Ben stayed in the top forty for ten weeks, he failed to qualify for the year's top-fifty best-selling singles, due in part to a

26 August: Kate Bush performs the opening night of twenty-two 'comeback' shows at London's Hammersmith

change in music-buying habits and the public's instant access to 'everything else'. 'Second Hand Heart', his follow-up single featuring Kelly Clarkson, entered the Official Chart at number twenty-one the following October, but slipped out of the top forty after just five weeks.

December 2014 also threw up a surprise Christmas number-one contender, with supporters of National League football side Wealdstone FC taking 'Got No Fans' by the Wealdstone Raider (aka vociferous supporter Gordon Hill) all the way to number five. Considerably less successful was a Facebook campaign to get Iron Maiden's 'The Number of the Beast' – previously a top-forty hit in 1982 and 2005 – to the number-one spot: the rock behemoths stalled at number forty-four.

NUMBER TWO
MARK RONSON FEAT. BRUNO MARS
'UPTOWN FUNK'

Any disappointment Mark Ronson and Bruno Mars felt when Ben Haenow knocked them off the top spot after just one week would have been short-lived when 'Uptown Funk' returned to number one for another six weeks – the longest stay of any chart-topper in 2015 and the best-selling single of that year.

2014
CHRISTMAS TOP TEN

1 Ben Haenow
'Something I Need'

2 Mark Ronson feat. Bruno Mars
'Uptown Funk'

3 Ed Sheeran
'Thinking Out Loud'

4 Olly Murs feat. Demi Lovato
'Up'

5 Wealdstone Raider
'Got No Fans'

6 Take That
'These Days'

7 Taylor Swift
'Blank Space'

8 One Direction
'Night Changes'

9 Calvin Harris feat. Ellie Goulding
'Outside'

10 Meghan Trainor
'All About That Bass'

'Uptown Funk' – the English DJ's first number one and the Hawaiian singer's fifth – included a songwriting credit for rapper Trinidad James, having sampled his 2012 single, 'All Gold Everything'. The credits also saw the later addition of brothers Charles, Robert and Ronnie Wilson of the Gap Band when it was agreed that elements of 'Uptown Funk' bore a similarity to their 1980 number-six hit, 'Oops Up Side Your Head'.

Apollo, her first concert in thirty-five years | 22 December: Singer Joe Cocker dies, aged seventy

THE CHRISTMAS HITS IN NUMBERS

PART II

12
Christmas number ones by US acts

14
Non-consecutive weeks at number one for Queen's 'Bohemian Rhapsody'

32
Christmas number ones that dropped to number two

35
Christmas number ones by solo artists

36
Characters in the longest Christmas number-one song title ('What Do You Want to Make Those Eyes at Me For?')

68
Weeks that Mariah Carey's 'All I Want for Christmas Is You' spent in the top forty before it got to number one

76
Weeks that 'Fairytale of New York' by the Pogues featuring Kirsty MacColl has spent in the top forty without getting to number one

77
Number of positions LadBaby fell in 2020 after topping the chart

15
Follow-up singles from Christmas number-one artists that also made number one

19
Christmas top-ten song titles containing fauna (an albatross, two ants, a buffalo, a bull, two crocodiles, a dog, two donkeys, an elephant, a goose, a monkey, a pigeon, a pup, a rooster, a wolf, and two unspecified birds)

30
Christmas number ones that were cover versions

43
Unique 'featured' artists on Christmas top-ten hits

50
Years of age of Cliff Richard when he claimed the 1990 Christmas number one (thirty-one years after his first chart-topper)

59
Number of unique acts to have had a Christmas number one

97
Length in seconds of Adam Faith's 1959 Christmas number two, 'What Do You Want?'

104
Total number of credited singers on Band Aid, Band Aid II and Band Aid 20

201
Total number of chart-toppers by Christmas number-one artists

952
Total number of combined weeks that Christmas number ones spent in the top forty

1104
Total number of top-forty hits by Christmas number-one artists

All figures correct as of May 2021.

Official Christmas Number 1

2015

LEWISHAM AND GREENWICH NHS CHOIR
'A BRIDGE OVER YOU'

WEEKS AT NUMBER ONE

1

Another product of reality TV, the Lewisham and Greenwich NHS Choir – like Christmas 2011's Military Wives – were formed for Gareth Malone's BBC TV series *The Choir*, finishing as 2012 runners-up to the choir from Severn Trent Water.

In 2013, the health service workers' ensemble released their blend of 'Bridge over Troubled Water'

(a 1970 number one for Simon & Garfunkel) and 'Fix You' (a 2005 number four for Coldplay), but it sold fewer than 5,000 units and failed to break into the Official Chart. Then, in 2015, doctors Katie Rogerson and Harriet Nerva and communications manager Joe Blunden launched a social media campaign to take the single to number one.

28 June: Tibetan spiritual leader the Dalai Lama makes an appearance at Glastonbury Festival |

Two weeks before Christmas, Justin Bieber was sitting at the top of the Official Chart with 'Love Yourself' – his third number one of the year and of all time. When the choir's campaign kicked off, 'A Bridge over You' and 'Love Yourself' were separated by fewer than 700 sales – that is until Justin took to social media himself and posted a message to his followers: 'For 1 week it's ok not to be #1. Let's do the right thing and help them win.' He also included a link for his fans to download the choir's single. When the Official Chart was announced on 25 December, 'A Bridge over You' was ahead by 30,000 units. Proceeds from its sale were split between causes including Carers UK and the mental health charity Mind.

NUMBER TWO
JUSTIN BIEBER
'LOVE YOURSELF'

When 'Love Yourself' by Justin replaced 'Sorry' by Justin at number one, the Canadian pop star became the first living act since the Beatles to achieve such a feat. (Refer back to 1963 for more on how 'I Want to Hold Your Hand' replaced 'She Loves You' to claim our Christmas top spot that year.) Prior to Justin, the late Elvis Presley posthumously replaced himself at the top when re-issues of 'Jailhouse Rock' and

2015
CHRISTMAS TOP TEN

1. **Lewisham and Greenwich NHS Choir**
'A Bridge over You'

2. **Justin Bieber**
'Love Yourself'

3. **Justin Bieber**
'Sorry'

4. **Adele**
'Hello'

5. **Justin Bieber**
'What Do You Mean?'

6. **Grace feat. G-Eazy**
'You Don't Own Me'

7. **Sigala feat. Bryn Christopher**
'Sweet Lovin''

8. **One Direction**
'History'

9. **Stormzy**
'Shut Up'

10. **Coldplay**
'Adventure of a Lifetime'

'One Night'/'I Got Stung' hit number one successively in January 2005.

Justin then made history on 8 January 2016 when 'Love Yourself', 'Sorry' and 'What Do You Mean?' – all previous number ones – comprised the top three positions on the Official Singles Chart.

1 August: Singer and TV presenter Cilla Black dies, aged seventy-two

Official Christmas Number 1

2016

CLEAN BANDIT FEAT. SEAN PAUL AND ANNE-MARIE
'ROCKABYE'

WEEKS AT NUMBER ONE
1

CLEAN BANDIT'S FOLLOW-UP SINGLE: 'SYMPHONY'
MARCH 2017

HIGHEST CHART POSITION 1

SEAN PAUL'S FOLLOW-UP SINGLE: 'BODY'
NOVEMBER 2017

HIGHEST CHART POSITION 76

ANNE-MARIE'S FOLLOW-UP SINGLE: 'CIAO ADIOS'
APRIL 2017

HIGHEST CHART POSITION 9

With no reality-TV backing, no maverick online campaign and no charity project to support it, 'Rockabye' became our first 'normal' Christmas number one since 'Mad World' by Michael Andrews and Gary Jules back in 2003.

While Clean Bandit had claimed their first number one with 'Rather Be' (featuring Jess Glynne) in 2014 and Jamaican rapper Sean Paul had featured on Blu Cantrell's 2003 number one, 'Breathe', and the Saturdays' chart-topping 'What About Us' in 2013, Anne-Marie was the new kid on the block, having only made her top-forty debut in August with 'Alarm'. On its third week in the Official Chart, 'Rockabye'

10 January: Singer and songwriter David Bowie dies, aged sixty-nine | 21 April: Singer and songwriter

overtook Little Mix's fourth number one, 'Shout Out to My Ex', to begin its nine-week stay at the top.

Seven weeks into its reign, 'Rockabye' became the first song in Official Chart history to be crowned Christmas number one after such a long spell in pole position. The record had previously been set by Frankie Laine in 1953 when 'Answer Me' topped the Yuletide chart after six weeks at number one. However, with sales spread across a longer period, the downside of Clean Bandit's extended stay at the top was that 'Rockabye' became the lowest-selling Christmas number one since Robbie Williams and Nicole Kidman's 'Somethin' Stupid' in 2001.

Clean Bandit would repeat the trusty 'featured artist' formula for their next two number-one singles: 'Symphony' in May 2017, featuring Zara Larsson, and 'Solo' in June 2018, featuring Demi Lovato.

NUMBER TWO
RAG'N'BONE MAN
'HUMAN'

Of the other nine artists in this year's Christmas top ten, six spent at least one week at number two behind Clean Bandit. Among them was Rory Charles Graham, aka Rag'n'Bone Man, whose Official Chart debut remained in the top

2016
CHRISTMAS TOP TEN

1. **Clean Bandit feat. Sean Paul and Anne-Marie**
'Rockabye'

2. **Rag'n'Bone Man**
'Human'

3. **Louis Tomlinson & Steve Aoki**
'Just Hold On'

4. **Little Mix**
'Touch'

5. **Mariah Carey**
'All I Want for Christmas Is You'

6. **Zara Larsson**
'I Would Like'

7. **The Weeknd feat. Daft Punk**
'Starboy'

8. **Matt Terry**
'When Christmas Comes Around'

9. **James Arthur**
'Say You Won't Let Go'

10. **Rae Sremmurd feat. Gucci Mane**
'Black Beatles'

ten for thirteen consecutive weeks, including three in the runner-up slot.

Despite that, 'Human' would end 2017 as the year's eighth best-selling single and Rag'n'Bone Man would win the British Breakthrough Act category and the Critics' Choice Award at the 2017 BRITs. So as not to spoil him, though, the organisers waited until 2018 before giving 'Human' the Single of the Year award.

Prince dies, aged fifty-seven | 25 December: Singer and songwriter George Michael dies, aged fifty-three

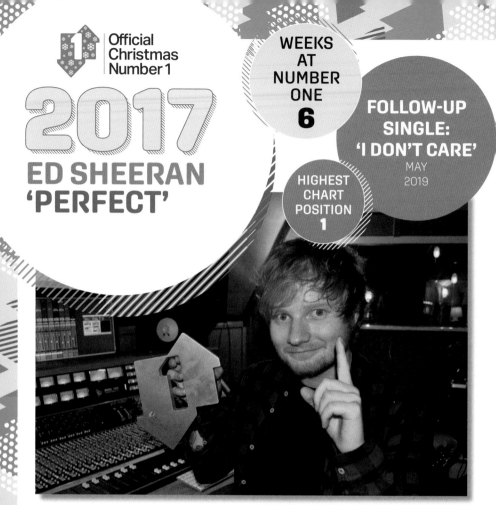

2017

ED SHEERAN 'PERFECT'

WEEKS AT NUMBER ONE
6

FOLLOW-UP SINGLE: 'I DON'T CARE'
MAY 2019

HIGHEST CHART POSITION
1

At the end of a phenomenal year that saw 'Shape of You' spend fourteen weeks at number one (its run only briefly interrupted by Harry Styles' solo debut, 'Sign of the Times'), Ed returned to the top spot in December with 'Perfect' – his fourth UK chart-topper. Not content with monopolising the Official Chart, though, Ed recorded a duet version of the song with Beyoncé that topped the US *Billboard* Hot 100 and an orchestral version with Italian tenor Andrea Bocelli ('Perfect Symphony') that gave him a toe in the classical charts, too. 'Perfect' would become the sixth best-selling single of both 2017 and 2018.

In March 2017, Ed broke two Official Chart records – Frankie Laine's 'four singles in the top ten

25 February: After twenty-seven years, DJ Brian Matthew presents his final episode of Radio 2's *Sounds of*

simultaneously' feat from 1953 and Justin Bieber's 'top-three places at the same time' accomplishment from 2016. This occurred when all sixteen songs from Ed's newly released third album, ÷, entered the top twenty concurrently, with nine of them in the top ten (the exception, number seven, went to 'Something Just Like This' by the Chainsmokers and Coldplay). As a result, Official Chart rules were changed to limit the number of top-100 songs per artist to three, so Ed's extraordinary feat is likely to remain unmatched.

'Perfect' spent six weeks at number one, only to be replaced by Ed again – this time in collaboration with rapper Eminem…

NUMBER TWO
EMINEM FEAT. ED SHEERAN 'RIVER'

Returning to one of our favourite and rarest Official Chart statistics: an artist replacing themselves at number one. It was only the fifth time such a phenomenon had happened, although Ed was just a 'featured' artist on this single by Eminem – the most successful rapper in Official Chart history. 'River' was Marshall Bruce Mathers III's ninth number one (having scored his first in 2000 with 'The Real Slim Shady') and his chart-topping hits have made a couple of appearances in our

2017
CHRISTMAS TOP TEN

1. **Ed Sheeran**
'Perfect'

2. **Eminem feat. Ed Sheeran**
'River'

3. **Wham!**
'Last Christmas'

4. **Mariah Carey**
'All I Want for Christmas Is You'

5. **Rita Ora**
'Anywhere'

6. **Big Shaq**
'Man's Not Hot'

7. **The Pogues feat. Kirsty MacColl**
'Fairytale of New York'

8. **Clean Bandit feat. Julia Michaels**
'I Miss You'

9. **Rak-Su feat. Wyclef Jean & Naughty Boy**
'Dimelo'

10. **NF**
'Let You Down'

previous Christmas top tens, too: 'Stan' in 2000 and 'The Monster', a collaboration with Rihanna, in 2013.

Moving away from all things Ed, 2017 saw Wham! and Mariah Carey together in the Christmas top ten for the first time, while the effect of streaming and voice-activated speakers meant that feeling festive no longer required even the touch of a button.

2018
LADBABY
'WE BUILT THIS CITY'

WEEKS AT NUMBER ONE
1

FOLLOW-UP SINGLE: 'I LOVE SAUSAGE ROLLS' DECEMBER 2019

HIGHEST CHART POSITION
1

After an eighteen-year wait, the first novelty song to claim the Christmas number-one slot since Bob the Builder's 'Can We Fix It?' finally arrived in the shape an ode to sausage rolls. Based on Starship's 1985 number-twelve hit, 'We Built This City' was released by blogger and social media star LadBaby (real name: Mark Hoyle), along with LadBabyMum (his wife, Roxanne) and their sons, Phoenix and Kobe. The single achieved first-week sales of 75,000 copies and its proceeds were donated to the Trussell Trust – a charity supporting a network of more than 1,200 UK foodbanks. Mark also won the (slightly less coveted) Celebrity Dad of the Year award in 2018, beating Rio Ferdinand, Prince William and Simon Cowell (a man who knows a thing or two about a Christmas number one).

Starship's original version was co-written by lyricist Bernie Taupin – long-term collaborator with

9 March: The final print edition of the *New Musical Express* is published | 14 June: Robbie Williams

Elton John. Bernie's partnership with Elton produced not only the UK's best-selling single of all time, 'Candle in the Wind 1997', but also the festive favourite 'Step into Christmas', as well as its lesser-known B-side, 'Ho, Ho, Ho (Who'd Be a Turkey at Christmas?)'.

From 1974 to 1984, Starship went by the name Jefferson Starship, having evolved from Jefferson Airplane – best known for their psychedelic anthem 'White Rabbit'. Though Jefferson Starship reached number twenty-one in 1980 with 'Sara', it was only under the name Starship that the American rock band scored their sole number-one hit – 'Nothing's Gonna Stop Us Now', taken from the soundtrack of the 1987 film *Mannequin*.

NUMBER TWO
AVA MAX
'SWEET BUT PSYCHO'

Ava's top-forty debut was co-written by Canadian Henry 'Cirkut' Walter, who previously had a talented hand in the 2013 number ones 'Roar' (Katy Perry) and 'Wrecking Ball' (Miley Cyrus).

In 2020, Ava collaborated on a Children in Need fundraising version of Oasis's 2002 single 'Stop Crying Your Heart Out', released under the name BBC Radio 2 Allstars. Among

2018
CHRISTMAS TOP TEN

1. **LadBaby**
'We Built This City'

2. **Ava Max**
'Sweet but Psycho'

3. **Ariana Grande**
'thank u, next'

4. **Mariah Carey**
'All I Want for Christmas Is You'

5. **Halsey**
'Without Me'

6. **Mark Ronson feat. Miley Cyrus**
'Nothing Breaks Like a Heart'

7. **Wham!**
'Last Christmas'

8. **Ariana Grande**
'imagine'

9. **Jess Glynne**
'Thursday'

10. **Post Malone feat. Swae Lee**
'Sunflower'

the artists featured on the track were former Christmas number-one alumni Robbie Williams, Melanie C (Spice Girls), Grace Chatto (Clean Bandit) and Kylie Minogue (Band Aid II). That same year, Ava also released her first Christmas single, 'Christmas Without You', but even the addition of sleigh bells and high notes from the Mariah Carey songbook were not enough to get it into the top 100.

performs at the opening ceremony of the 2018 FIFA World Cup in Russia

2019

LADBABY
'I LOVE SAUSAGE ROLLS'

WEEKS AT NUMBER ONE
1

FOLLOW-UP SINGLE: 'DON'T STOP ME EATIN''
DECEMBER 2020

HIGHEST CHART POSITION
1

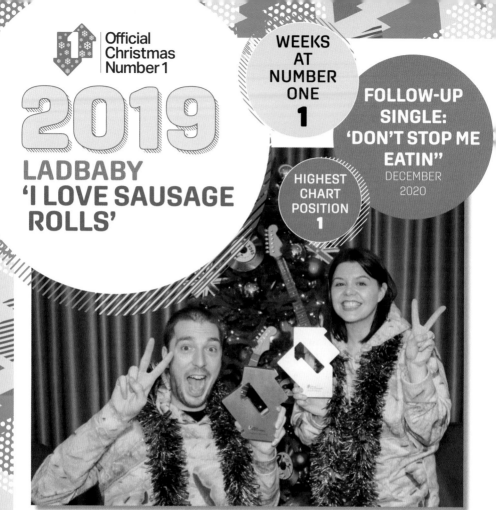

A welcome return for Mark 'LadBaby' Hoyle and family, whose second release in aid of foodbank charity the Trussell Trust made them the first act to achieve back-to-back novelty Christmas number ones. Video production values were increased to incorporate an inflatable sausage roll, matching sausage roll jumpsuits and a sausage roll guitar, which clearly worked for the UK music-buying public, as sales were up 23 per cent on the previous year. Meanwhile, following Mark's 2018 parenting success, Roxanne 'LadBabyMum' Hoyle was crowned Celebrity Mum of the Year 2019, beating off competition from Kate Middleton, Holly Willoughby and the Saturdays' Rochelle Humes.

18 May: The UK's Michael Rice finishes last at the Eurovision Song Contest | 2 July: A peak audience

In its original (meat-free) form, 'I Love Rock 'n' Roll' began life as a B-side, featuring on the Arrows' 1975 single 'Broken Down Heart' – a release that failed to add to the pop band's tally of two top-forty hits. Four years later, American singer Joan Jett – previously with rock band the Runaways – recorded the song as the B-side to her debut solo single, 'You Don't Own Me'. She then re-recorded it for her 1981 album, also called *I Love Rock 'n' Roll*, and the single spent three weeks at number four when it was released the following year. A 2002 version by Britney Spears also performed well, peaking at number thirteen that November and becoming the thirteenth top-forty single of her thirty-strong total.

NUMBER TWO
STORMZY FEAT. ED SHEERAN & BURNA BOY
'OWN IT'

Another Christmas runner-up that would make its way to number one in the New Year, 'Own It' was the second collaboration between rapper Michael 'Stormzy' Owuo Jr and Edward 'Ed' Sheeran. (The first, 'Take Me Back to London', spent five weeks at number one earlier in the year.) Joining the pair on the single was Nigerian rapper Burna Boy – a serial collaborator whose top-forty

2019
CHRISTMAS TOP TEN

1. **LadBaby**
   'I Love Sausage Rolls'
2. **Stormzy feat. Ed Sheeran & Burna Boy**
   'Own It'
3. **Lewis Capaldi**
   'Before You Go'
4. **Dua Lipa**
   'Don't Start Now'
5. **Wham!**
   'Last Christmas'
6. **Stormzy feat. Headie One**
   'Audacity'
7. **Arizona Zervas**
   'Roxanne'
8. **Mariah Carey**
   'All I Want for Christmas Is You'
9. **Stormzy**
   'Lessons'
10. **Tones and I**
    'Dance Monkey'

hits have seen him share the credits with Dave, Jorja Smith, J Hus, and Headie One.

The Christmas top ten also saw Wham!'s 35-year-old festive favourite, 'Last Christmas', returning for a third consecutive year, partly helped by a limited-edition, 7-inch, white vinyl re-issue that topped the Official Vinyl Singles Chart with almost 5,000 sales.

THE BIGGEST-SELLING CHRISTMAS NUMBER ONES

We will all have our own favourite Christmas number one, usually linked to a personal story or time and place, but there is only one way to judge the entire nation's festive favourites – by reviewing the all-time best-seller lists compiled by the Official Charts Company.

Officially, the UK's biggest Christmas number one ever is Band Aid's 'Do They Know It's Christmas?', which was the festive chart-topper in 1984 and has now sold 3.8 million copies. It is an incredible statement of that song's popularity that Band Aid 20 also features in the official all-time list at number fifteen.

Not far behind Band Aid is Queen's 'Bohemian Rhapsody' – the only recording on the list that has been Christmas number one twice, first in 1975 and again in 1991 (latterly as a double A-side with 'These Are the Days of Our Lives').

Strangely, Wings' third-place 'Mull of Kintyre' ranks higher in the all-time list than any of the Beatles' three Christmas number ones, although the Fab Four can claim three of the top ten biggest sellers of all time.

The most recent of the tracks in the top twenty is Alexandra Burke's 2008 chart-topper, 'Hallelujah'. This should not be too much of a surprise, though, given how few singles are sold today. Most music fans now rely on streaming.

As a result, our list of the most-streamed Christmas number ones is very different, although there is some crossover.

Counting all-time plays of songs on all of the key streaming services (including Amazon, Apple, Spotify, YouTube and many more), the most-streamed track of the lot is Ed Sheeran's 'Perfect', having racked up more than 400 billion streams in the four years since it was released. The second most-streamed track is 'Bohemian Rhapsody', just ahead of Clean Bandit's 'Rockabye' – both with less than half of Ed's total.

The two charts displayed here count all-time sales and streams, dating from release until the end of May 2021.

OFFICIAL BIGGEST-SELLING CHRISTMAS NUMBER ONES

3.83 million	'Do They Know It's Christmas?' Band Aid
2.62 million	'Bohemian Rhapsody'' Queen
2.09 million	'Mull of Kintyre'/'Girls' School' Wings
1.90 million	'Mary's Boy Child/Oh My Lord' Boney M.
1.82 million	'I Want to Hold Your Hand' The Beatles
1.67 million	'I Will Always Love You' Whitney Houston
1.65 million	'Don't You Want Me' Human League
1.43 million	'I Feel Fine' The Beatles
1.41 million	'Day Tripper'/'We Can Work It Out' The Beatles
1.33 million	'Hallelujah' Alexandra Burke
1.32 million	'Merry Xmaƨ Everybody' Slade
1.27 million	'Green, Green Grass of Home' Tom Jones
1.22 million	'Earth Song' Michael Jackson
1.19 million	'Mary's Boy Child' Harry Belafonte
1.19 million	'Do They Know It's Christmas?' Band Aid 20
1.16 million	'Another Brick in the Wall (Part II)' Pink Floyd
1.15 million	'2 Become 1' Spice Girls
1.12 million	'That's My Goal' Shayne Ward
1.05 million	'Can We Fix It?' Bob the Builder
1.02 million	'When We Collide' Matt Cardle

© Official Charts Company

OFFICIAL MOST-STREAMED CHRISTMAS NUMBER ONES

403 billion	'Perfect' Ed Sheeran
190 billion	'Bohemian Rhapsody'' Queen
188 billion	'Rockabye' Clean Bandit feat. Sean Paul and Anne-Marie
131 billion	'Merry Christmas Everyone' Shakin' Stevens
126 billion	'Do They Know It's Christmas?' Band Aid
89 billion	'Merry Xmaƨ Everybody' Slade
71 billion	'I Will Always Love You' Whitney Houston
68 billion	'Don't You Want Me' Human League
52 billion	'Killing in the Name' Rage Against the Machine
51 billion	'Stay Another Day' East 17
48 billion	'Mary's Boy Child/Oh My Lord' Boney M.
43 billion	'Another Brick in the Wall (Part II)' Pink Floyd
43 billion	'Lonely This Christmas' Mud
41 billion	'Hallelujah' Alexandra Burke
31 billion	'Mistletoe and Wine' Cliff Richard
29 billion	'I Want to Hold Your Hand' The Beatles
27 billion	'Always on My Mind' Pet Shop Boys
26 billion	'Something I Need' Ben Haenow
25 billion	'Sound of the Underground' Girls Aloud
23 billion	'2 Become 1' Spice Girls

© Official Charts Company

2020
LADBABY
'DON'T STOP
ME EATIN''

WEEKS AT NUMBER ONE
1

In 2020, LadBaby became the first act since the Spice Girls to score three consecutive Christmas number ones, although LadBaby's chart-toppers hung around for a total of just four weeks, while the Spice Girls' three spent a combined thirty-three weeks in the top forty.

Nevertheless, sales for LadBaby's third offering were again significantly up on the previous year – helped in part by a remix featuring Ronan Keating – and they landed the best-selling Christmas number one since Ben Haenow's 2014 debut.

'Don't Stop Believin'' (the basis of 'Don't Stop Me Eatin'') was originally recorded by American rock band Journey for their 1981 album, *Escape*. Although *Escape* topped the *Billboard* album chart and gave the band four US top-twenty singles, UK audiences were a tougher nut to crack and 'Don't Stop Believin'' got no further than number sixty-two in the Official Chart.

In 2007, it crept back in at the bottom end of the top 100 after featuring in the finale of TV drama *The Sopranos*, but its more significant return occurred two years later when Joe McElderry – our 2009 Christmas 'runner-

30 January: The first two known cases of COVID-19 in the UK are confirmed in York | 6 November:

up' – performed the song on *The X Factor*, pushing Journey up to number six in the Official Chart. Perhaps Journey's original would have done even better were it not for a thunder-stealing a cappella cover by the cast of US TV show *Glee*, although there were four weeks at the beginning of 2010 when both versions co-existed in the UK top ten simultaneously.

The success of 'Don't Stop Me Eatin'' meant that, at the end of 2020, LadBaby became the second act (after Robson & Jerome) whose entire Official Chart career consisted of just three number-one singles.

NUMBER TWO
MARIAH CAREY
'ALL I WANT FOR CHRISTMAS IS YOU'

After sixty-nine weeks in the top forty, including four years when it peaked at number two, Mariah's festive hit finally claimed the number-one slot in December 2020, staying there for two weeks until LadBaby took over on Christmas Day.

Similarly, after sixty-two weeks in the top forty, including two years when it peaked at number two, Wham!'s 'Last Christmas' finally topped the Official Chart on New Year's Day 2021.

2020
CHRISTMAS TOP TEN

1 **LadBaby**
'Don't Stop Me Eatin''

2 **Mariah Carey**
'All I Want for Christmas Is You'

3 **Wham!**
'Last Christmas'

4 **Jess Glynne**
'This Christmas'

5 **The K**ts**
'Boris Johnson is a F**king C**t'

6 **The Pogues feat. Kirsty MacColl**
'Fairytale of New York'

7 **Shakin' Stevens**
'Merry Christmas Everyone'

8 **Justin Bieber**
'Rockin' Around the Christmas Tree'

9 **Band Aid**
'Do They Know It's Christmas?'

10 **Elton John**
'Step into Christmas'

However, our sympathies still lie with the Pogues and Kirsty MacColl. Although 'Fairytale of New York' has racked up seventy-four weeks in the top forty across eighteen different years, it has somehow managed to spend at least a week at every position in the top twenty except number one.

Cliff Richard becomes the first artist to have a top-five album in eight consecutive decades

LOOK TO THE FUTURE NOW, IT'S ONLY JUST BEGUN...

Music, particularly Christmas music, continues to be a source of comfort, joy and – in the case of the Christmas number-one single – speculation, made all the more special and fascinating by the fact that the result is so wonderfully unpredictable.

We have seen time and time again that trends and previous sales history can count for nothing and that even the most sophisticated and expensive marketing campaigns can be upstaged by the power of people and events.

And we don't seem to tire of Christmas classics. Instead, they get put away with the decorations and ignored for ten or eleven months, only to be greeted like old friends the following year and taken to our hearts once again. There is no spring or Easter equivalent and – with all due

respect to Stevie Wonder and Altered Images – nothing for birthdays either.

We could muse that the Christmas number one is the result of people wanting to have fun, but then how do we explain 2003's 'Mad World'? Some festive hits present us with the opportunity to think of others, but then where does Mr Blobby fit in? If the focus is on Christmas party classics, then why don't any of LadBaby's three chart-toppers fill the dancefloor? It can no longer be the case that the Christmas number one is the perfect stocking-filler when 99 per cent of 'sales' are actually streams.

The Official Chart has changed and evolved to reflect what we are buying and how we are buying it. Recent years have seen the introduction of dedicated charts for audio streams, vinyl singles, rock and metal, hip-hop and R&B, Afrobeats, indie and even classically inspired songs. In the US (where chart data also includes the number of times a song is played on the radio), *Billboard* magazine compiles a weekly 'Holiday 100' in November and December to track the popularity of Christmas songs. At the end of 2020, though, these 'holiday hits' occupied thirty-nine places in the main Hot 100. Could we see a similar thing in the UK? As Pete Waterman says within these pages, 'something will come along'.

For almost seventy years, the Official Chart music elves have been gathering data for us to dissect, discuss and share. We are reliably informed that they have their 'finger on the throbbing pulse of the British record-buying, digital-downloading, music-streaming public'. Their hard work has informed the hundreds of titles featured in this book; it has given us the opportunity to dig up old facts worth repeating, unearth trivia that deserves a wider audience, and make new, interesting and hopefully not too obvious musical connections.

Armed with all this information, are we now better placed to spot the next Christmas number one and predict which favourites will return to the top ten? Perhaps – though maybe better placed than most is the presenter of *The Official Chart* on Radio 1, Scott Mills, whose words we will leave you with:

"

The first Christmas record I remember buying was Shakin' Stevens' 'Merry Christmas Everyone'. I played it and played it and played it and played it. That's why songs like that are still around: people of my age remember loving them back in the day and now they've all got kids, so their kids love them, too.

In recent years, lots of classic Christmas songs have returned to the charts – Slade, Wizzard, Wham!, Mariah Carey. There's not as much appetite for the newer songs, at least not yet, but that's because the classic songs mean so much to all the family.

Many of the songs are very British, too – not known overseas. We have actually tested this out on my radio show. There's a service in America called Dial-A-Carol, which you can call 24/7 during the Christmas period and they will sing you a Christmas song. Every year, we call up and ask for the Pogues or Wizzard or 'Last Christmas' and they offer us 'Rudolph the Red-Nosed Reindeer' instead.

I feel very honoured to be able to announce the Christmas number one. It is a special moment, a uniquely British phenomenon and something we should always keep hold of.

"

SO THIS IS QUIZMAS...

MULTIPLE CHOICE

1. The Bing Crosby song 'White Christmas' was written by Irving Berlin for which film, released in 1942?
   a) *Winter Inn*
   b) *Holiday Inn*
   c) *Berni Inn*

2. On the original 1984 version of 'Do They Know It's Christmas?' by Band Aid, who sang the opening line?
   a) Bob Geldof
   b) Bono
   c) Paul Young

3. According to the Waitresses' 'Christmas Wrapping', what did singer Patty Donahue 'forget' and have to visit the all-night grocery to pick up?
   a) Carrots
   b) Crackers
   c) Cranberries

4. The 1972 single 'Merry Xmas (War Is Over)' is credited to John & Yoko and the Plastic Ono Band with the ... ?
   a) Boys of the NYPD Choir
   b) Harlem Community Choir
   c) Band of the Coldstream Guards

5. The video for Wham!'s 'Last Christmas' was filmed in which Swiss ski resort?
   a) Saas-Fee
   b) St Moritz
   c) Tobe-le-Rhône

6. What was the B-side of Benny Hill's Christmas number one, 'Ernie (The Fastest Milkman in the West)?
   a) 'The Dustbins of Your Mind'
   b) 'Ting-A-Ling-A-Loo'
   c) 'Gather in the Mushrooms'

7. 'When Christmas Comes Around', the 2016 debut single for *X Factor* winner Matt Terry, was co-written by Amy Wadge and which Christmas number-one artist?
   a) Leon Jackson
   b) Michael Jackson
   c) Ed Sheeran

8. Which Christmas number-one artist referred to the idea of Rage Against the Machine claiming the 2009 top spot as 'kind of funny'?
   a) Paul McCartney
   b) Alexandra Burke
   c) Mark 'LadBaby' Hoyle

9. Having topped the Christmas chart in 1983, the Flying Pickets made another attempt the following year with a cover of which Eurythmics hit?
   a) 'Who's That Girl?'
   b) 'Sweet Dreams (Are Made of This)'
   c) 'Love Is a Stranger'

10. Nicole Kidman, who duetted on our 2001 Christmas chart-topper, was born in the same city as the artist who featured on our 2014 Christmas number two. What birthplace do they share?
    a) Sydney, Australia
    b) Honolulu, Hawaii
    c) Las Vegas, Nevada

TRUE OR FALSE?

11. Al Martino, our first-ever Christmas number-one artist, has four children, three of whom are also called Al.

12. The Christmas number-one artists Winifred Atwell and St Winifred's School Choir are the only Winifreds to ever appear in the Official Singles Chart top forty.

13. The Beatles' second chart-topper, 'She Loves You', was replaced at number one by 'Bad to Me' – a song by Billy J. Kramer with the Dakotas that was written by John Lennon and Paul McCartney.

14. The Scaffold, our 1968 Christmas chart-toppers, recorded a version of Baddiel, Skinner and the Lightning Seeds' 'Three Lions', but changed the title to '3 Shirts on a Line'.

15. The Christmas 1972 top ten included 'Little' Jimmy Osmond at number one and his brother Donny at number nine, both of whom have played the title role in the musical *Joseph and the Amazing Technicolor Dreamcoat*.

16. Wizzard's 'I Wish It Could Be Christmas Everyday' originally included a credit for 'additional noises' by 'Miss Snob and Class 3C'.

17. Bob Heatlie, writer of Shakin' Stevens' 'Merry Christmas Everyone', also wrote the theme tune for the ITV quiz show *Wheel of Fortune*.

18. 'Babe', Take That's 1993 Christmas number two, was the theme song from an Oscar Award-winning film about a pig that learns how to herd sheep.

19. Mark 'LadBaby' Hoyle and his wife Roxanne 'LadBabyMum' Hoyle named their two sons after their local football team, Nottingham Forest.

20. 'A Bridge over You', our 2015 Christmas number one by the Lewisham and Greenwich NHS Choir, is a combination of the 'Love Can Build a Bridge' (a 1995 number one for Cher, Chrissie Hynde & Neneh Cherry with Eric Clapton) and 'Over You' (a 1980 number five for Roxy Music).

TOP-FORTY TRIVIA

21. The 1980 Christmas number one, 'There's No One Quite Like Grandma', is one of just two top-forty hits containing the word 'Grandma'. The other, 'Grandma's Party', was a number-nine hit in 1976 for which singer?

22. Which Liverpudlian act had two singles in the Christmas 1965 top ten, including that year's best-selling single in the UK?

23. 'Wombling Merry Christmas' was the biggest of five top-forty hits for the Wombles in 1974, four of which had a play on the word 'Womble' in the title. The odd one out was titled after what type or flavour of 'rock'?

24. Which '70s Christmas favourite includes instrumental elements from Russian composer Sergei Prokofiev's 1934 'Lieutenant Kijé' suite?

25. Name the former Eurovision Song Contest winner who had a Christmas top-ten hit with 'It's Gonna Be a Cold Cold Christmas'.

26. Which vocal 'group' accompanied Paul McCartney on his 1984 Christmas top-ten hit, 'We All Stand Together'?

27. Name the comedian and film director who followed up his 1987 Christmas top-ten hit with the 1991 single 'Another Blooming Christmas'.

28. Jess Glynne had a 2020 top-ten hit with 'This Christmas' – a song that has also been covered by Gloria Estefan, the Temptations, and the Four Tops – but which US soul legend wrote the song?

29. Which TV personality scored four top-forty hits between 1993 and 1998, including a number-seven duet with Elton John, but stalled at number sixty-one with his cover of festive favourite 'Little Drummer Boy'?

30. In 1988, which Christmas classic helped Bros land the fifth of their eleven top-forty hits?

31. Twenty years before the department store became a player in the Christmas chart race, which other John Lewis was responsible for a 1980 Christmas number three?

32. 'The Perfect Year', Dina Carroll's Christmas 1993 top-ten hit, was originally written for which Andrew Lloyd Webber musical?

33. Which singer, actress and TV personality went straight to number one with her debut album, but can only boast one top-forty single – a 1998 number ten, aptly titled 'Cruise into Christmas'?

34. In 2003, the music video for which Christmas top-ten hit included appearances from Bob Geldof, Holly Valance, Spice Girl Melanie B, Atomic Kitten's Kerry Katona, and All Saints' Melanie Blatt?

35. 'See the Day' has twice been a Christmas top-ten hit, most recently for Girls Aloud in 2005, but who originally took the song to number three in 1985?

36. Whose cover of 'Seven Little Girls Sitting in the Back Seat', a 1959 Christmas top-ten hit for the Avons, entered the Official Chart in December 1990?

37. What un-festive two-word phrase provided the title for Christmas top-ten hits by the Black Eyed Peas (2003) and Stormzy (2015)?

38. Which TV duo took Kylie and Jason's 1988 Christmas number two, 'Especially for You', back into the Christmas top ten a decade later?

39. 'I Only Want to Be with You' has been in the Christmas top ten twice: first for Dusty Springfield in 1963, then for which new-wave quintet in 1979?

40. Mark Ronson has charted in the Christmas top ten on three occasions, each time with a different singer: Amy Winehouse in 2007; Bruno Mars in 2014; and which other chart-topping artist in 2018?

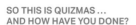

SO THIS IS QUIZMAS …
AND HOW HAVE YOU DONE?

ANSWERS

1. *Holiday Inn*
'White Christmas' won an Oscar for Best Original Song at the fifteenth Academy Awards in March 1943. Also nominated were 'I've Got a Gal in Kalamazoo', from the film *Orchestra Wives*, and 'There's a Breeze on Lake Louise', from *The Mayor of 44th Street*.

2. Paul Young
Songwriters Bob Geldof and Midge Ure wanted David Bowie to sing the opening line, but he was unavailable for the 25 November recording session. He did sing the line at the 1985 Live Aid concert, though.

3. Cranberries
The Waitresses' festive favourite has never reached any higher than number forty-five on the UK Official Singles Chart, but it was streamed more than 2 million times in 2020 alone.

4. Harlem Community Choir
'Happy Xmas (War Is Over)' was released in 1971 in the US, where it peaked at number forty-two, but we had to wait twelve months for its UK release.

5. Saas-Fee
In addition to George, Andrew and backing singers Pepsi and Shirley, the video featured model and actress Kathy Hill as George's ex-girlfriend. At the time, Kathy was dating Greek musician Vangelis – a Christmas top-ten artist in 1981 with 'I'll Find My Way Home' by Jon & Vangelis.

6. 'Ting-A-Ling-A-Loo'
'The Dustbins of Your Mind' was the B-side of 'Fad Eyed Fal', Benny's 1972 single, and 'Gather in the Mushrooms' was his 1961 Official Chart debut.

7. Ed Sheeran
The single also features a choir, with vocal arrangements by Ed's brother, Matthew.

8. Paul McCartney
Paul told Sky News: 'If [Joe McElderry] goes to number one, then good luck to him … I've got nothing against that, but it would be kind of funny if Rage Against the Machine got it.'

9. 'Who's That Girl?'
The Flying Pickets' version peaked at number seventy-one on 2 December 1984.

10. Honolulu, Hawaii
Both Nicole and 'Uptown Funk' singer Bruno Mars (real name: Peter Hernandez) were born in Hawaii's capital, Honolulu. Nicole made her film acting debut in the 1983 drama *Bush Christmas*.

11. True
Al Martino's four children are Alfred Cini (Al's birthname), Alana Cini, Debbie Martino and Alison Martino.

12. True
'Lullaby of Broadway' by Winifred Shaw did reach number forty-two in 1976, though. She originally recorded the song for the musical film *Golddiggers of 1935*.

13. False
It was the other way around: 'She Loves You' actually replaced 'Bad to Me' at number one, although the latter indeed was a Lennon and McCartney composition.

14. True
The Scaffold's version of 'Three Lions' was recorded for *Liverpool – The Number Ones Album*, a compilation of twenty-one chart-topping singles by Liverpudlian artists covered by other artists from Liverpool.

15. True
Other number-one artists who have played Joseph include David Cassidy, Jason Donovan, Stephen Gately of Boyzone, Joe McElderry and Gareth Gates.

16. True
The label of the original 7-inch single read: 'Vocal backing by the Suedettes, plus the Stockland Green Bilateral School first year choir. Additional noises Miss Snob and Class 3C.'

17. True
And the presenter of *Wheel of Fortune*, DJ Nicky Campbell, also presented *Top of the Pops* between 1988 and 1996.

18. False
The theme song from *Babe* was 'If I Had Words', originally a number-three hit in 1978 for Scott Fitzgerald and Yvonne Keely. In the film, it was sung by actor James Cromwell, as well as by a trio of mice.

19. True
Mark and Roxanne's two boys are Kobe Notts Hoyle and Phoenix Forest Hoyle.

20. False
'A Bridge over You' is a combination of 'Bridge over Troubled Water' (a 1970 number one for Simon & Garfunkel) and 'Fix You' (a 2005 number four for Coldplay).

21. Paul Nicholas
The British singer and actor – star of the BBC sitcom *Just Good Friends* – had four top-forty hits, including the 1976 number eight 'Dancing with the Captain'.

22. Ken Dodd
The Liverpudlian comedian and singer was at number three and number five in the Christmas top ten with 'The River' and 'Tears', respectively. The latter was the UK's best-selling single of the year and the third best-selling single of the decade.

23. Banana
'Banana Rock', the Wombles' third successive top-ten hit, peaked at number nine. Just in case buyers forgot who they were listening to, though, the single's B-side was 'The Womble Square Dance'.

24. 'I Believe in Father Christmas' by Greg Lake
Our 1975 Christmas number two quotes Prokofiev, though the single's B-side was a slightly less festive instrumental entitled 'Humbug'.

25. Dana
The singer born Rosemary Brown won the 1970 Eurovision Song Contest with 'All Kinds of Everything' – the first success in the competition for Ireland.

26. Frog Chorus
'We All Stand Together' is credited to Paul McCartney and the Frog Chorus, though the B-side – a 'Humming Version' of the song – lists his backing group as the Finchley Frogettes.

27. Mel Smith
The follow-up to 'Rockin' Around the Christmas Tree', Mel's number-three duet with Kim Wilde, was 'Another Blooming Christmas', from the soundtrack to the film adaptation of Raymond Briggs' *Father Christmas*.

28. Donny Hathaway
Both of his UK top-forty hits were duets with Roberta Flack: 'Where Is the Love' made number twenty-nine in 1972 and 'Back Together Again' peaked at number three in 1980.

29. RuPaul
The star of *RuPaul's Drag Race* had his biggest hit with 'Don't Go Breaking My Heart', a remake of Elton's 1976 number-one duet with Kiki Dee.

30. 'Silent Night'
A double A-side release with 'Cat Among the Pigeons', this was one of four Bros singles that stuck at number two. Lucky buyers of the limited-edition 7-inch single were treated to a free set of Bros Christmas stickers.

31. Jona Lewie
John Lewis (aka Jona Lewie) spent five weeks at number three in December 1980 and January 1981 with 'Stop the Cavalry'.

32. *Sunset Boulevard*
The lyrics for the musical were written by Don Black, who was also the lyricist behind 'Ben', Michael Jackson's 1972 Christmas top-ten hit.

33. Jane McDonald
The star of BBC documentary *The Cruise* had a total of eight top-forty albums between 2000 and 2020, but remains a one-hit wonder in the Official Singles Chart.

34. 'Proper Crimbo' by *Bo' Selecta!*
Following this number-four hit, comedian Leigh Francis returned to the Official Chart in 2004, in the company of Davina McCall and Patsy Kensit, with a number-five version of 'I Got You Babe'.

35. Dee C. Lee
It was the only solo top-forty hit for the former Wham! backing singer and Style Council member.

36. Bombalurina
It was the follow-up to their August 1990 number one, 'Itsy Bitsy Teenie Weenie Yellow Polkadot Bikini', which had originally been a number-eight hit for Brian Hyland in 1960.

37. 'Shut Up'
The Black Eyed Peas' third top-forty hit peaked at number two in December 2003, while Stormzy's single reached number eight in December 2015. The same title also provided different hits for Madness in 1981 and Kelly Osbourne in 2003.

38. Denise and Johnny, aka Denise van Outen and Johnny Vaughan
The pair were co-presenters on Channel 4's *The Big Breakfast* at the time. Denise had a second top-forty hit in 2002 when she recorded a version of 'Can't Take My Eyes Off You' with Andy Williams.

39. The Tourists
Featuring future Eurythmics Annie Lennox and Dave Stewart, the Tourists took their version of 'I Only Want to Be with You' to number four – the same spot as Dusty Springfield's version sixteen years earlier.

40. Miley Cyrus
Mark and Miley's 'Nothing Breaks Like a Heart' peaked at number two, as did 'Valerie', his 2007 collaboration with Amy Winehouse. 'Uptown Funk', featuring Bruno Mars, is Mark's only UK number one to date.

ACKNOWLEDGEMENTS

Additional material written by Martin Talbot and Rob Copsey at the Official Charts Company and by Pete Selby at Nine Eight Books.

All UK chart positions and sales figures reproduced by kind permission of the Official Charts Company and their indispensable officialcharts.com website.

Search 'Official Charts' on all good streaming platforms for the 'Every Official Christmas Number 1 Ever' playlist.

Michael Mulligan would like to thank:

Pete Selby and Melissa Bond at Nine Eight Books for their encouragement, guidance and patience.

Dr Pete Waterman for once again sharing his extraordinary knowledge and enthusiasm.

Friends and colleagues at record labels and in record shops for advice, support and the occasional curry.

Sarah, who provided endless support, love, affection, tea and cake, and the Tommos, for morale-boosting chocolate.

Dedicated to my mother, who turned on that small transistor radio on the mantlepiece every morning.

Nine Eight Books would also like to thank Fiona Greenway, Alex May at Bonnier Books UK, Martin Talbot and Lauren Kreisler at the Official Charts Company, Graham Betts, and Sophy Henn for early creative support.

CREDITS AND DISCLAIMER

Credits

pp. 8, 10, 14, 18, 20, 30, 40, 42, 56, 58, 60, 92 – Pictorial Press Ltd/Alamy Stock Photo; p. 12 – Everett Collection Inc/Alamy Stock Photo; p. 22 – Michael Levin Photography/Alamy Stock Photo; p. 24 – PixMix Images/Alamy Stock Photo; p. 28 – World History Archive/Alamy Stock Photo; p. 32 – PictureLux/Hollywood Archive/Alamy Stock Photo; pp. 34, 126, 134, 136 – Trinity Mirror/Mirrorpix/Alamy Stock Photo; p. 36 – Tribune Content Agency LLC/Alamy Stock Photo; p. 44 – TCD/Prod.DB/Alamy Stock Photo; p. 46 – Tim Mander/Alamy Stock Photo; p. 48 – Kay Roxby/Alamy Stock Photo; p. 54 – Ian Tyas/Keystone Features/Getty Images; p. 62 – Gijsbert Hanekroot/Alamy Stock Photo; p. 66 – David Pimborough/Alamy Stock Photo; pp. 68, 84, 124 – United Archives GmbH/Alamy Stock Photo; p. 70 – David Redferns/Redferns/Getty Images; p. 72'– Sovfoto/Universal Images Group/Shutterstock; p. 74 – Moviestore Collection Ltd/Alamy Stock Photo; p. 80 – ANL/Shutterstock; pp. 82, 144 © supplied by Globe Photos, Inc/Globe Photos/ZUMAPRESS Inc/Alamy Stock Photo; p. 86 – George Richardson/Landmark/MediaPunch/Alamy Stock Photo; p. 88 Realimage/Alamy Stock Photo; p. 94 Album/Alamy Stock Photo; pp. 96, 110, 122 – AF archive/Alamy Stock Photo; p. 98 – David Lichtneker/Alamy Stock Photo; pp. 100, 128 – Dave Hogan/Hulton Archive/Getty Images; p. 106 – Alan Olley/TV Times/Future Publishing via Getty Images; p. 108 – Terry Dean/Alamy Stock Photo; pp. 112, 138, 140, 148, 160 – PA Images/Alamy Stock Photo; p. 114 – dpa picture alliance/Alamy Stock Photo; p. 118 – Martin Beddall/Alamy Stock Photo; p. 120 – Lehtikuva/Shutterstock; p. 132 © Nickelodeon, courtesy of Everett Collection/Alamy Stock Photo; p. 146 – Tim Roney/Getty Images; pp. 150, 152 – WENN Rights Ltd/Alamy Stock Photo; p. 158 – EDB Image Archive/Alamy Stock Photo; p. 164 – Dan Goldsmith/TV Times/Future Publishing via Getty Images; pp. 162, 166, 170, 172, 174, 176, 178, 182 – Official Charts Company; p. 185 © Nicky Johnston

Disclaimer

We hope you enjoy this definitive guide to the history of that very British institution: the official Christmas number one. This is a unique collaboration between the Official Charts Company, Michael Mulligan and Bonnier Books' new music imprint, Nine Eight Books.

In compiling this book, we have plundered the depths of the chart archives right back to 1952. Over those seventy years, the process of chart compilation has changed beyond measure – from the telephone poll of twenty record shops in November 1952 to the present-day counting of audio streams, video streams, track downloads, vinyl sales, CD purchases and other physical formats via automated data delivery and aggregation.

Throughout that period, the publication day of the chart has changed several times, too. In recent years, the recognised chart date is the last date that the chart is live. However, in earlier decades, the date followed the publication date of the newspaper or magazine in which the chart was published – be that the *New Musical Express* (with an original publication day of Friday), *Record Retailer* (with a publication day of Saturday) or *Music Week* (also a Saturday).

Additionally, in these modern times, the Christmas number one is occasionally announced on Christmas Day itself – as was the case in 2020. Conversely, back in the 1950s, the chart was often given a rest for the week over Christmas because of the logistical challenges posed by the closure of record shops and unreliable postal services. Furthermore, the charts in those early days were primarily distributed in print magazines and newspapers, rather than via the instant communication methods we have in today's world of national radio broadcasters, global internet access and international social media networks.

For these reasons, the further back we travel in time, the more complex the process of compiling historic chart data becomes. Broadly, we have opted to adhere to the rules that were applied at the time – our aim being to reflect the charts as they were published, read and experienced contemporaneously. That said, where we have become aware of errors in the published charts, we have made corrections whenever it has been possible and logical to do so.

We are fully aware that no database of this size and complexity can be 100 per cent perfect, but we have striven to ensure that it is as accurate as it possibly can be. Please also note that all data included within this book was correct at the time of writing (May 2021). If you have any questions or queries about our data (or would just like to send us fan mail!), please feel free to get in touch via email: feedback@officialcharts.com.